THE UNITED TOUR
—OF—
MANCHESTER

THE UNITED TOUR
—OF—
MANCHESTER

Iain McCartney & Tom Clare

AMBERLEY

First published 2013

Amberley Publishing
The Hill, Stroud
Gloucestershire, GL5 4EP

www.amberley-books.com

British Library Cataloguing in Publication Data.
A catalogue record for this book is available from the British Library.

ISBN 978 1 4456 1913 2 (print)
ISBN 978 1 4456 1918 7 (ebook)

Typesetting and Origination by Amberley Publishing.
Printed in Great Britain.

Contents

Introduction

Today, Manchester United is not simply a football club, but a worldwide institution: a global brand on a parallel with the likes of Coca-Cola and Apple. It is a scenario far removed from their formative years when they were nothing more than a 'works team', a number of enthusiastic individuals with a binding, similar interest.

From Newton Heath to Manchester United, they survived bankruptcy and the threat of extinction, the destruction of their third home at the hands of the German Luftwaffe and, the hardest blow of all, the loss of eight players in the 1958 Munich disaster.

J. H. Davies and James Gibson are names that few will recognise now, but their part in the United story cannot be ignored; likewise, the post-war rebuilding of the team by Matt Busby and his able assistant Jimmy Murphy, who laid the foundations for what we have today. But upon those foundations, which for short periods of time were far from firm and secure, a towering edifice was slowly constructed by a certain Alex Ferguson, whose tenure at Old Trafford has created the Manchester United that we see today. But for him, there would not be the stadium or indeed the list of honours that we can proudly boast about.

Over the years, the history of Manchester United has been well documented, recalling the players and the games from the past, the highs and the lows. What you are holding and reading now, however, is a Manchester United history with a difference. Yes, it tells you about the pioneering players from the Newton Heath depot of the Lancashire & Yorkshire Railway Carriage and Wagon Works, the attempt to solve the financial problems that beset the club, the disaster on that slush-covered German runway, and the club as it is today. But this particular book takes you beyond the pages of any previous publication and indeed, beyond the walls of the club's excellent museum within the bowels of Old Trafford itself.

It takes you onto the streets of Manchester, to places you will have read about. To the exact location where the railway workers kicked that first ball in earnest on North Road Newton Heath. It follows them from the smelly surroundings of Clayton to Old Trafford. Ever wondered where Sir Matt Busby is buried? Only a throw-in away from another United legend, Billy Meredith, as it happens. There are also the graves of Munich victims Eddie Colman and Geoff Bent to be found, along with other monuments and buildings of note that are associated with Manchester United. This book takes you on the 'United Tour of Manchester'.

Who knows what you will discover?

In the Beginning

The Lancashire & Yorkshire Railway Company grew out of the Manchester & Leeds Railway, changing its name in 1847 after a series of amalgamations with other companies, purchasing both the East Lancashire Railway and the West Lancashire Railway companies. Connecting Lancashire & Yorkshire via the Pennines, the Lancashire & Yorkshire Railway was then able to link Liverpool and Manchester with York and Goole, and also served Bolton, Wigan, Blackpool, Lytham, Barnsley, Bradford, and Huddersfield. The company became responsible for the third-largest railway system based in Northern England (after the Midland and North Eastern Railways) and the largest network entirely within Northern England.

The huge size and intensity of the company was reflected in the rolling stock that it owned, which included some 1,650 locomotives. Their railway system was the most densely trafficked system within the British Isles and had more locomotives per mile than any other company. The company also operated an incredible 1,904 passenger services, a figure only exceeded by the Midland Railway Company.

Obviously, to facilitate and service all of the different sections of the company a huge infrastructure was needed, and part of that was the Locomotive, Carriage, and Wagon Works. Initially, this was situated in the suburb of Miles Platting, which is just over a mile to the north of Manchester's city centre. However, in 1873, a huge fire at this site completely devastated the works buildings and area, rendering it redundant. This led to the development of a new complex just a mile further north from the Miles Platting site, situated on North Road, Newton Heath. Four years later, in 1877, the new site of the Lancashire & Yorkshire Railway Carriage and Wagon Works, a large sprawling complex that stretched further northwards and across Thorp Road (employing between 800 and 900 people) was complete.

The Carriage and Wagon Works on North Road got into full operation immediately, and the workers were blessed not only with the finest of work tools needed to complete their tasks but also with superior working conditions compared to many at that time. The *Manchester Guardian* reported on 24 January 1878:

Of great magnitude combining in their arrangements everything necessary for rapid production with all the conveniences that the most watchful solicitude could suggest for the comfort of the workpeople, embracing the newest and most perfect appliances, exhibiting the perfection of method and the highest class of workmanship, finished with rare taste and skill – the Newton Heath Railway Carriage Works, in small things as in great, are a practical application of the excellent maxim that anything worth doing is worth doing

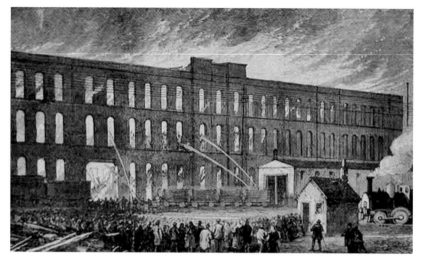

A print showing the Lancashire & Yorkshire Railway Carriage and Wagon Works fire in Miles Platting, Manchester, 1873.

well. It will probably be urged that this latter has hardly been the guiding principle of the Lancashire & Yorkshire Railway in times past.

We now come to a most interesting feature in its economy. Nearly half the workforce eats their meals on the premises. For their convenience a handsome dining room that will seat some 500 persons, has been provided, with a spacious kitchen and lavatory adjoining. The Company has placed in the kitchen a couple of men cooks, who see to the warming of dinners, or to the cooking of any unprepared food brought by the men. It will be readily imagined where the diners and the dishes are so numerous that the arrangements must not only be extensive but also complete, and the kitchen is well appointed. In the dining room the tables and seats are all numbered, and each man has his place. The Company find the table cutlery and certain tin platters, and in return for these conveniences each man contributes one penny per week to a fund which goes not to the Company but for the providing of newspapers and which will ultimately be the means of furnishing the works with a library. The dining room is managed by a Dining-Room Committee consisting of a certain number of foremen, and a certain number of men, elected by the general body of employees.

They have in their hands the selection of newspapers and the like, and they exercise a wide impartiality of political opinion. During the time in which the men are taking their dinner, they hear from the lips of one of their number the most important news of the day. The reader taking up any journal he likes selects such items of intelligences as he thinks of most interest, and if he is wise in his selections, though he read but imperfectly, he can always command the attention of his hearers.

The men appoint the reader weekly, and the arrangement, which we have seen practiced in certain college 'refectories' for the excellent purpose of preventing idle and fruitless gossip, seems to answer well. At the weekend, the newspapers are put up for auction in the dining room, and are readily purchased by the workmen.

The *Guardian* article also went on to say, 'It should be stated that in the Upholstery Department, a considerable number of women are employed, and that in their rooms – which are quite removed from those of the men – they enjoy similar advantages.'

Within such a huge workforce, countless friendships were made and what leisure time that was available to those hard-grafting individuals was regularly spent in many of the local drinking establishments. Simultaneously, those with similar interests began to look at forming small organisations and soon the Carriage and Wagon Works had a thriving social scene.

Before the new Factory Act was passed in 1847, workers had very little time for leisure or pleasure. Due to their long working hours, most people were far too busy trying to make ends meet to think overmuch about enjoying themselves. If you work fourteen or fifteen hours a day in a factory, there is precious little time left for anything other than eating and sleeping. The new Factory Act implemented a full ten-hour working day for workers of both sexes and all ages. Although still not ideal, it was certainly a start, and self-improvement, education, sports and pastimes began to take their rightful place in people's lives. Workers now had the ability to watch and take part in sport, especially football that was now available to the masses.

Geoffrey Green, in his wonderful book *There's Only One United* (Hodder & Staughton, 1978, page 192), refers to a letter that he received during his research from the secretary of the Newton Heath Loco Football Club – a club quite separate and distinct from the one about to be formed. The secretary's letter stated that 'the old Lancashire & Yorkshire Railway started what were known as "Improvement Classes" in 1859, from which the workers formed sports clubs.'

Activities requiring the kicking of a ball date back many centuries. Indeed, the earliest archaeological evidence relates to a military manual dating back to the second and third centuries BC in China and the playing of a game named *cuju*. Although there is documented evidence that a form of ball game was played in Britain as far back as the eighth century, the sudden acceleration of the game of association football as we know it did not occur until the middle of the nineteenth century. The Cambridge Rules, first drawn up at Cambridge University in 1848, were particularly influential in the development of subsequent codes, including association football. The Cambridge Rules were written at Trinity College, Cambridge, at a meeting attended by representatives from Eton, Harrow, Rugby, Winchester, and Shrewsbury schools. They were not universally adopted. During the 1850s, many clubs unconnected to schools or universities were formed throughout the English-speaking world to play various forms of football. Some came up with their own distinct sets of rules, most notably the Sheffield Football Club formed by former public school pupils in 1857, which led to formation of a Sheffield FA in 1867. In 1862, John Charles Thring of Uppingham School also devised an influential set of rules.

These ongoing efforts contributed to the formation of the Football Association (FA) in 1863, which first met on the morning of 26 October 1863 at the Freemason's Tavern in Great Queen Street, London. The only school to be represented on this occasion was Charterhouse. The Freemason's Tavern was the setting for five more meetings between October and December, which eventually produced the first comprehensive set of rules.

At the final meeting, the first FA treasurer, the representative from Blackheath, withdrew his club from the FA over the removal of two draft rules at the previous meeting: the first allowed for running with the ball in hand; the second for obstructing such a run by hacking (kicking an opponent in the shins), tripping and holding. Other English rugby football clubs followed this lead and did not join the FA, or subsequently left the FA and instead in 1871 formed the Rugby Football Union.

The eleven remaining clubs, under the charge of Ebenezer Cobb Morley, went on to ratify the original thirteen laws of the game. These rules included handling of the ball by 'marks' and the lack of a crossbar – rules which made it remarkably similar to Victorian rules football being

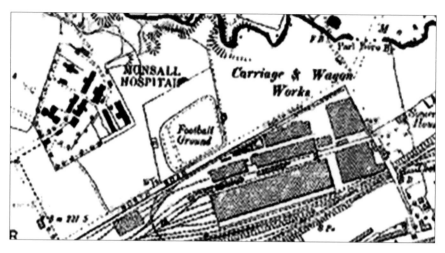

A map of
the football
ground.

developed at that time in Australia. The Sheffield FA played by its own rules until the 1870s, with
the FA absorbing some of its rules until there was very little difference between the games.

At the Newton Heath Carriage and Wagon Works, one organisation that was established was
the Dining-Room Committee, the idea of the Works Chief Superintendent and Engineer, a Mr
Frederick Attock. Attock was born in Liverpool on 10 February 1842, but shortly after his birth,
the family moved to Essex, where his father became superintendent of the Great Eastern Railway
Carriage and Wagon Department. It followed that his son would be apprenticed to him, and he
eventually succeeded him in his post in 1874.

In early 1877, following the retirement of Charles Fay, Attock moved to Manchester to assume
the position of Carriage and Wagon Superintendent of the Lancashire & Yorkshire Railway.
He was a compassionate man, always had the health and welfare of his workers at heart and
consequently was extremely popular with the workforce.

With football gaining popularity, it was not surprising that members of the workforce, and
indeed those of the Dining-Room Committee, should take an interest in the sport, and at some
time in 1878 (there is no record of the actual date) members of the Dining-Room Committee
approached Mr Attock and asked him if it would be possible for them to form their own football
team. Attock was enthusiastic about the idea, but first the workers had to have a field upon which
they could play the game. An ideal site was soon located close by; a small plot of land, across
North Road, and facing the Carriage and Wagon Works, which was owned by the Manchester
Cathedral authorities.

Attcock was again approached and he was successful in persuading the Lancashire &
Yorkshire Railway Company to negotiate a nominal rent for the use of the land, and when this
was accomplished, they leased the land to the newly formed association football club. The name
of the new football club was Newton Heath (L&YR) Football Club

Never in their wildest dreams from such a humble beginning could the railway company,
Mr Attock, or the workers themselves have ever have envisaged that what they had founded
would turn into the football and commercial juggernaut that is Manchester United today.

North Road, 1878

Leaving Manchester's city centre, you begin your journey by traveling east along Oldham Street and then cross the junction with Great Ancoats Street. Proceed up Oldham Road (A62) and travel eastwards towards Oldham. Cross the junction with Queens Road and Hulme Hall Lane and continue towards Oldham. Pass Monsall Road on the left-hand side and then, just 300 yards further on, turn left into the Gateway. Cross over the railway bridge and immediately on the left- and right-hand sides are the grounds of what used to be the Lancashire & Yorkshire Railway Carriage and Wagon Works. As you approach the roundabout, take the second exit into Central Park also known as the North Manchester Business Park (M40 5BP). This is the site of what was the North Road Football Ground, first home of the Newton Heath (LY&R) Football Club.

The North Road acreage, where the Newton Heath (LYR) football team played its first fixtures, was owned by the Manchester Cathedral authorities. It was situated on what is now Northampton Road, Newton Heath, and the Central Business Park stands on what used to be the old football ground. In 1878, the Lancashire & Yorkshire Railway Company were able to negotiate a nominal rent for the land with the church authorities, but they in turn leased the plot to the newly formed works football team. Upon first sight, the North Road playing field was anything but a surface conducive to playing football upon. It was a grassless, uneven, stone-ridden piece of land.

The History of Lancashire Football Association (Blackburn: Tomlin, 1928) described it as 'in places it was as hard as flint, with ashes underneath that had become like iron, and in others, thick with mud'. In the souvenir programme printed for the Newton Heath FC fund raising bazaar held at the St James Hall, Oxford Street, Manchester, in 1901, there is a description of North Road and it says:

> The ground was little more than a clay pit, its surroundings a quagmire. After you had entered the bottom gate it was quite a work of art to steer clear of the pools of water. But once you got there, you were alright – if it didn't rain. If it did – well, if you have never experienced it, you cannot possibly be enlightened.

The elected Dining-Room Committee was a very proactive part of the Carriage and Wagon Works. In addition to a football team, they also formed a cricket team, a choir, a brass band, and an athletics team. They would encourage workers to take part in many activities and most of the concerts, athletics meetings and other outdoor activities, would take place upon the North Road ground.

For the football team, in 1878, the facilities were very sparse. There were no changing rooms of any type and the players had to get changed in the Three Crowns public house, which was on nearby Oldham Road, and later at the Shears Hotel which was the club's headquarters. The latter public house was some half a mile away from North Road and for the players it meant a leisurely jog to the ground before and back again at full-time. There were no stands on the land, and initially facilities for the spectators were just as sparse as they were for the players. They would stand shoulder to shoulder and many deep alongside the touchlines and goal lines to watch a match. In

Left: Northampton Road sign.

Above: Ceylon Street, Newton Heath.

inclement weather, the ground was nothing more than a mud-heap that often went almost ankle deep. The spectators were kept from trespassing on to the playing area by means of ropes attached at various distances to wooden pickets that were stretched around all four sides of the pitch. It is estimated that there was capacity for some 12,000 bodies.

There is no real record of the very first matches played at North Road as football was very rarely reported upon in the local press. It is more departmental in basis, and there was no real structure to the games with the workers playing the game in their normal everyday clothing. Another team was formed from the men who worked as engine drivers for the company and this was named Newton Heath Locomotive whose ground was at Ceylon Street. Quite often the mistake is made of identifying the 'Loco' as the precursor to Manchester United.

Newton Heath (L&YR) Football Club's first playing strip was a green-and-gold halved shirt that were the colours of the company. Frederick Attock the Works Superintendant was also able to persuade such notable local dignitaries as MPs A. J. Balfour (who later went on to become Prime Minister), C. E. Schwann, and Sir James Fergusson, plus the *Manchester Guardian* newspaper editor, C. P. Scott, as vice presidents of the club.

The Newton Heath club was to play at North Road for some fifteen years (1878–93) and during that time there were a number of changes that took place to improve the ground, mainly forced upon them due to their popularity and progression in the growing football arena of the time. The earliest recorded attendance of 3,000 was for a game against West Gorton St Marks on 12 November 1881. This is the first recorded 'derby' fixture between what is now Manchester United and Manchester City, as the Gorton team grew into the club that eventually became Manchester City. For the note, Newton Heath were the victors in that first encounter by 3-0. It was not until the mid-1880s, as the club rose up the football ladder and their fixture list became more attractive, that attendances began to increase, and with that came the need for new and better facilities for the spectators.

In the early days the gate charge was 3*d*, but by those mid-1880s years, it had risen to 6*d*. Professionalism had now started to appear in the game, with many players being paid 'under the counter', and Newton Heath could also add the inducement to attract good players by not only paying them, but giving them jobs in the Carriage and Wagon Works and also offering them concessionary railway travel. It was at this time that attendances began to fluctuate between 3,000 and 8,000 and the club fast became the most successful club in the Manchester area.

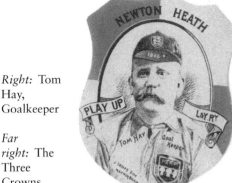

Right: Tom Hay, Goalkeeper

Far right: The Three Crowns Hotel.

There was also the beginning of a distance between the football club, and the company whose name they carried. When the Football League was formed in 1888, the Newton Heath club was desperate to gain membership to what was then termed as the elite, as far as club football was concerned. However, during those early years, the League authorities rejected application after application, and the club had to be content to play their Football Alliance fixtures as well as many friendly matches. The club committee was ambitious, and in 1891 two new stands were built upon the football ground, enhancing the small structures that had first been built in 1887. In 1892, the Football League absorbed the Football Alliance into their fold, and there was a reorganisation of the League into two separate divisions – a First and a Second Division.

When the reorganisation took place, together with Nottingham Forest and The Wednesday (later to become Sheffield Wednesday), Newton Heath were added to the elite clubs in the First Division. The dream at last had been realised, but with it came the problems.

The connections with the Lancashire & Yorkshire Railway Company were finally severed and the football club was formed into a limited company. Immediately, the railway company reacted by withdrawing the arrangement for concessionary rail travel and also raised the rent for the North Road football ground. Obviously, the club's progression into League football brought added expense and the club had to find ways of raising revenue to try and stay solvent. A share issue was realised but proved to be more than a little disappointing. Then came the bombshell.

During the summer of 1893, Newton Heath was served with an eviction order by the company to vacate their North Road home. There had been complaints from the company's cricketers that football was ruining the ground for them to pursue their summer activity. But the main reason was that the Cathedral authorities were not happy that the football club was charging admission for spectators to watch their games. The land had been leased to the company for use by all of the railway workers, and by charging an admission price, the club was denying those workers the right to use the facility. It broke the terms of the lease with the company. It was a little bit two-faced really, because the company only paid the religious authority a nominal sum for their lease while on the other hand, they received a rent of over £500 per season from the club and they pocketed the profit. The club was ordered to leave their North Road home before the start of the 1893/94 football season. They were also told to leave the ground as they had found it or forfeit their new stands. The club had little option and had to leave them behind, receiving from the company less than £100 – a considerable financial loss.

Above left: Newton Heath *v.* The Canadians team sheet.

Above right: A football ground stood on this site for a number of years in the 1800s. A team played in Newton Heath called Ten Acres, and they are presumed to have played on this site. Local rumour also suggests that, prior to the officially recognised incorporation of Newton Heath L&YR in 1878, the club played some games on Ten Acres Lane in an unofficial capacity, possibly as early as 1875. This will probably never be proven, however on 10 May 1890 Newton Heath lost a home fixture 4-0 to Preston North End, in front of 6,000 people, on Ten Acres Lane.

Below: North Manchester Business Park on Northampton Road, Miles Platting, Manchester, showing the Japanese Fujitsu Company's buildings, which now sit on the original site of North Road, Manchester United's first home.

The last game ever played by Newton Heath Football Club (they dropped the L&YR part of the club's name upon their formation as a limited company) was on 8 April 1893. It was a League game against Accrington Stanley that resulted in a 3-3 draw before 3,000 spectators. The highest recorded attendance at a game at North Road came just four weeks before that final game, when 15,000 spectators watched Sunderland demolish Newton Heath in a First Division game by 5-0. During the close season, the new secretary of the club, Mr Alf Albut, and the committee members frantically searched for a new home for the club. They were eventually successful when towards the end of June 1893 they came across a ground not too far away in the area of Clayton, Manchester, which was owned by the Bradford & Clayton Athletic Company. The second new dawn in Manchester United's great history was about to begin.

Before proceeding to Newton Heath's second home, there is a slight detour to make. Go back down The Gateway and turn left onto Oldham Road (A62) and continue until you see Old Church Street on the right. Take a right again, just past Newton Heath Library (M40 2JB) and proceed along Millwright Street (M40 2QZ), turning left onto Duncan Edwards Court. Here we find a number of small blocks of houses, named after the players who lost their lives at Munich, along with a commemorative plaque.

Right: The Shears Hotel.

Below left: The sign for Duncan Edwards Court.

Below right: Newton Heath Library mural.

> MILLWRIGHTS STREET
> LEADING TO
> TOMMY TAYLOR CLOSE
> EDDIE COLMAN CLOSE
> BILLY WHELAN WALK
> GEOFF BENT WALK
> ROGER BYRNE CLOSE
> DAVID PEGG WALK

Above: A sign showing housing developments named after the United players killed at Munich.

Left: Munich air disaster plaque.

CITY OF MANCHESTER

On 6th February, 1958, a tragic air crash occured which has become known throughout the world as the 'Munich Air Disaster'. Among those who lost their lives were eight members of the Manchester United Football Team, affectionately known as the 'Busby Babes'.

Their loss to the Club and to the world of association football was immense but, like a phoenix Manchester United rose from the ashes of Munich to be F.A. Cup Finalists in the same season as the Disaster and ultimately to resume their place as one of the world's great football clubs.

It was able to do so largely due to the courage and tenacity of its Manager, Sir Matt Busby Kt., C.B.E., K.C.S.G. and the inspiration which he gave to others.

•——•——•——•——•

This development and the streets which surround it are named in recognition of the historical links between the Newton Heath area and the Manchester United Football Club and to commemorate those young players who so tragically lost their lives on that fateful day –

> Geoff Bent
> Roger Byrne (Captain)
> Eddie Colman
> Duncan Edwards
> Mark Jones
> David Pegg
> Tommy Taylor
> Billy Whelan

Sir Matt Busby unveiled this plaque on 16th May, 1983 in the twenty-fifth anniversary year of the disaster

Bank Street, Clayton

Return the way you have just come and turn left, back onto Oldham Road and just before your previous route along The Gateway, take a left into Ten Acres Lane. Proceed along Ten Acres Lane and cross the junction with Briscoe Lane. The road begins to twist and turn and you will pass Clayton Vale on the left, and then Phillips Park Cemetery on the right. The road becomes Banks Bridge Road and then becomes Bank Street. Continue along until you come to the National BMX Centre (M11 4DQ) on the right-hand side – this was the site of the former Bank Street Football Ground.

For Secretary Albut and the Newton Heath Football Club officials, the early summer months of 1893 became a frantic effort to find a new home for the club. Evicted from their North Road home, the club had to be ready by the first week in September to start their Football League

Division One campaign with a home fixture against Burnley. Approaches to the Cathedral authorities brought instant rebuttal, and things looked bleak as they scoured every spare patch of land in Manchester. It was a difficult task as none of the lots they looked at had the facilities to host a top Football League club.

Finally, at the end of June 1893, they found what they were looking for. It was a stadium owned by the Bradford and Clayton Athletic club, situated some 3 miles to the south of North Road and on Bank Street in the Clayton area of Manchester – but it was at least a football pitch. There was an initial meeting with the Bradford & Clayton Recreative Committee and an amicable agreement between the two parties was negotiated. Newton Heath Football Club was able to rent the ground for eight months of the year, with a couple of nights a week earmarked for training purposes.

At first, Bank Street seemed to provide the ideal location. The stadium was larger than North Road and could therefore attract bigger attendances. Facilities were much better. There was a Main Stand that ran alongside one side of the ground, and between the months of June through August, Albut and the committee and groups of volunteers worked to update it. There was also a small stand on the opposite side that was also renovated. The playing surface was far better than had been at North Road and at the beginning of the 1893/94 season it had a grass surface. When the time came for the first game to be played on 2 September, everything looked to be in good order.

The Manchester Courier reported on 4 September 1893:

> Newton Heath opened their new ground with a League match against Burnley, before a large attendance. The Committee had many difficulties before they secured the ground at Bank Lane, Clayton, which is held by the Bradford and Clayton Athletic Company Limited. They have been treated very well by the Athletic Company, and every possible assistance has been rendered by them. The playing portion of the ground is in splendid condition, and will probably prove to be as fast as any ground in the country. It was in reference to stands that a great amount of work was required, and no effort has been spared since they got the ground into their hands to get ready for Saturday's match; they have not been quite successful, but before the next first-team fixture there will be accommodation for several thousand more. There is one big stand nearly the full length of the ground, divided into several portions, for different ticket holders; besides this there is another stand behind the goal at the Bradford end, while at the Clayton goal the ground has been banked up, room for some thousands thus provided. This terracing ought to be carried along the side of the ground opposite the stand, and then the popular side will be complete.

The Manchester Courier also reported that there was an attendance of some 7,000 spectators present when the game kicked off, and it was to be a happy start for the club at their new home when they were victors over the Burnley team by 3-2.

The move, while presenting the club with the possibility of additional revenue, meant the team were now no longer 'Newton Heath' when it came to the geographical side of things, and in 1894 they applied to change their name to 'Manchester FC' This move, however, was blocked by a rugby club of the same name, who plied their trade in Whalley Range and who complained to the Rugby Union as regards Newton Heath's proposed plans. For the time being at least, the tenants of Bank Street had to remain as Newton Heath FC.

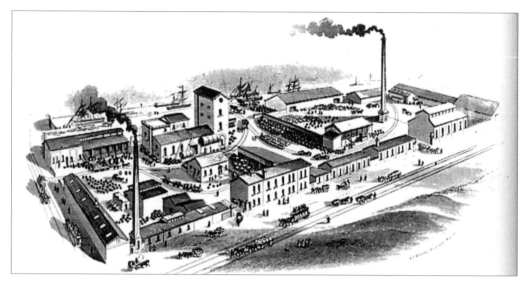

A sketch of the Clayton Aniline Company premises.

Despite the *Manchester Courier* painting such a rosy picture of the ground, it turned out to be anything but. The Manchester suburb of Clayton was a built up industrialised area, with many factories surrounding the dark, damp, terraced houses that people who worked for the companies lived in. At the back of one of the Bank Street stands, was the Ashton Canal (it is still there today) and on the other side of it was a very large chemical company named the Clayton Aniline Company. Founded by French chemist Charles Dreyfus in 1876, the company manufactured dyestuffs, aniline salts, and aniline oil, which were produced for the local calico printers. Two towering chimneys within the company grounds belched out toxic, acrid smoke and fumes over the local area including the ground, and these were joined by no fewer than thirty other large chimneys in the Clayton area, all belonging to dye manufacturers, cotton mills, collieries, brick kiln works, and engineering companies.

So the east side of Manchester was not a very good area to be, but Newton Heath was to stay at Bank Street for some seventeen years. It was not unusual during football matches for the smoke from the chimneys to drift into the ground, making it difficult for both players and spectators to see. Visiting teams complained – especially if they had been beaten! The foul atmosphere found itself canonised in rhyme:

As Satan was flying over Clayton for Hell,
He was chained in the breeze, and likewise the smell.
Quoth he; 'I'm not sure in what country I roam,
But I'm sure by the smell I'm not far from home.'

The playing surface quickly turned into a quagmire during the winter months and at times the players were ankle deep in mud. But nonetheless, Bank Street played such an important part in both Newton Heath's and Manchester United's history. During those seventeen years it saw the club almost bankrupt and drift into extinction in 1902. It saw the club change its name from Newton Heath to Manchester United, and it saw the club win its first major honours – the Football League

Above: An FA Cup game against Arsenal being played at Bank Street, Clayton, on 10 March 1906. Note the Clayton Aniline factory chimneys towering above the Main Stand with the spectators on the roof.

Right: A letterhead showing the Bank Street address.

Below left: Ravensbury Street.

Below right: Opposite this plaque was the Bank Street Ground.

Division One trophy in 1908, and the FA Cup in 1909. Along the way the ground was graced by so many names entrenched in the history of the club among them Albut, Stafford, John Henry Davies, Ernest Magnall, Billy Meredith, Charlie Roberts, Dick Duckworth, Alec Bell, Georgie Wall, 'Sandy' Turnbull, Harry Moger, and Louis Rocca. The occupation of Bank Street from 1893 until 1910 saw periods of elation, despair, sheer doggedness, intrigue, and finally success. But once the club left Bank Street for Old Trafford, it would be another thirty-eight years before the club would lift another major trophy.

The last League game played at Bank Street was a Division One fixture against Tottenham Hotspur on 22 January 1910 and just as they had started back in September 1893, the club would end with a victory by 5-0. The *Manchester Guardian* reported on 24 January 1910, 'the spectators did not number more than five thousand, and thus the last League game at Clayton ended in United recording their biggest win of the season in the presence of about the smallest crowd that ever assembled there'.

The third chapter in Manchester United's history was about to begin.

Manchester City Centre: The Grand Hotel, Aytoun Street

It was here on 20 September 1926 that an FA Commision held an enquiry into 'Certain affairs connected with the United club'. A further meeting in Sheffield followed a week later, and the following month it was then announced that the United manager, J. A. Chapman, had been suspended for the remainder of the season for 'Improper Conduct'.

To this day, what the 'improper conduct' charge has never been revealed. Chapman, considered a gentleman by all who knew him, in an interview with the *Topical Times* magazine, admitted his surprise at the FA's decision and that he had no idea as to what the charge meant or inferred. He also felt that he still had the backing of 'the big majority' of the United board. He added:

> I have nothing whatsoever on my conscience. I have worked conscientiously for Manchester United, and apart from my salary, I can say honestly that I have never benefited a single penny piece in any shape or form. There are numerous occasions upon which I have, in the interests of the club, been out of pocket, but that is a mere detail. I cannot possibly discuss the matters that came before the Commission.
>
> But I will say this that I considered them to be purely domestic, and merely concerned the club itself, and these dated back to more than a season ago.

Mentioning that he had the backing of 'the big majority' of the board suggests that within the club someone had an axe to grind and reported Chapman to the Football Association.

Some twenty-odd years later, Alf Clarke of the *Manchester Evening Chronicle*, writing in his history of the club, published in 1948, revealed that he knew full well of what had transpired, but would only say that a player was involved in the matter. To this day, the exact details have never been revealed. It is one of the most mysterious events in the club's history.

Chapman walked away from football and he was replaced by United's only ever player-manager, Clarence Hilditch, who served that post until the arrival of Herbert Bamlett the following season.

The Grand Hotel today.

The Grand Hotel as it was.

The hotel is now an apartment building and few will know about the building's United connection, although many older supporters will be familiar with Aytoun Street, as it was from here that the 'match day' special buses would leave for Old Trafford.

Leaving Aytoun Street, head towards Piccadilly station on London Road and opposite the main entrance to the station is the Malmaison Hotel. Opened in 1998, the hotel stands on the site of the old Joshua Hall warehouse, but upon the hotel forecourt once stood the Imperial Hotel. It was one of a number of hotels in the city owned by Mr J. H. Davies, under the Walker and Homphrey banner, and as you can see from the flag fluttering in the breeze on the postcard opposite, it was also the one time headquarters of United. The player whose portrait is displayed on its walls is club captain Harry Stafford, who was actually gifted the pub by Davies in 1901, but who lasted little time behind the pumps, declaring that this was not the life for him!

The hotel, while part of United's history, is also a part of Football League history, as it was here that the first meeting of the Players Union was held by Charlie Roberts and his United colleagues, Billy Meredith, Charlie Sagar, Herbert Burgess and Sandy Turnbull on 2 December 1907. Also at the meeting were players from Manchester City, Newcastle United, Bradford City, West Bromwich Albion, Notts County, Sheffield United, and Tottenham Hotspur. Jack Bell, the former chairman of the Association Footballers' Union (AFU) also attended.

The pub survived until as late as the 1980s before being demolished. The site was redeveloped with the old Joshua Hoyle warehouse next door becoming the Malmaison Hotel, which opened in 1998. The pub itself occupied what is now the hotel forecourt.

Above: Fans boarding buses on Aytoun Street.

Below left: The Imperial Hotel.

Below right: The Malmaison Hotel.

St James Hall, Oxford Street

St James Hall, Oxford Street, was the site of a fundraising bazaar for the ailing Newton Heath FC in 1901.

It was held over four days from Wednesday 27 February, and the brochure issued for the event mentions that it had been organised 'to raise sufficient funds to place the club on a sound financial basis and which could enable the management to obtain a team capable of securing and maintaining a position in the First Division of the Football League'. It was hoped to raise around £1,000.

Opened by the MP for Manchester North East, Sir James Fergusson, the event featured music from Besses o' the Barn brass band and the Northern Military. Visitors were free to wander around looking at exhibits, including scenes of India, Italy and the Mediterranean, while Major the St Bernard dog, owned by club captain Harry Stafford, did the same, collecting donations in a box strapped to his collar.

While the bazaar itself made very little profit after the costs of hiring the hall, etc., were taken into consideration, Major's involvement proved more beneficial, although the true story surrounding the St Bernard's involvement is clouded through the mists of time. One story recalls how he wandered out of the hall and somehow found his way to a public house owned by brewery owner Mr J. H. Davies. His daughter immediately took a liking to the dog and when Stafford heard where his pet was, and went to claim it, Davies offered to buy it from him. Stafford is reported as telling Davies that he loved his dog and also loved his football team and if the Brewery boss was to pump money into Newton Heath, then he would sell him the dog. To this Davies agreed.

A number of years later, the daughter who wanted the dog said in an interview:

The dog was wandering along Oxford Road, after escaping from a Dog Show and was taken to my father's office in St Anne's Place. It was later claimed by Harry Stafford and my father asked him if he would sell him the dog, as I wanted it. Stafford said 'no', as the dog had saved his life at Blackpool, when he had jumped in to save a bather who had got into difficulties with cramp. (Obviously the dog must also have jumped into the sea.) The dog was later awarded a Royal Humane Society Medal.

The latter part of that story is certainly untrue, as such a medal has never been awarded!

Another story, as related by Louis Rocca, mentions that the dog was locked in an upper room of the hall, and that he was on nightwatchman duty with another when they heard a noise and when they went to investigate and opened a door, the dog rushed out. Rocca also gives the name of the dog as 'Ruby'! This tale is very unlikely to be true.

But back to the bazaar, which unfortunately made very little profit. However, the incident with the dog was to prove more profitable than the bazaar could ever have hoped to have been.

The building was demolished just a few years later and replaced by the Calico Printers building, which still stands and is now also referred to as St James Hall.

While on Oxford Street, heading towards Central Library, is The Alibi pub. So, where does this fit into the history of Manchester United, other than being a pre-/post-match watering hole for

Above: Newton Heath FC brochure cover, 1901.

Left: St James Hall.

Below: St James Hall, Oxford Street, as it is today.

The Plaza today.

members of the Red Army? The building has certainly changed since those halcyon days of the fifties, when it was, even then, a meeting place for the young at heart, coming under the name of the Plaza Ballroom. The Plaza was a well-known haunt of the 'Babes' and is regarded as one of the first disco venues in the country, where the DJ was none other than a certain Jimmy Saville.

The flamboyant record spinner would often recall how the younger members of Busby's team could often be found on the edge of the dancefloor, with numerous young ladies hoping that they would catch the footballers' eyes and be asked to dance.

Leaving Oxford Street, we turn onto Lower Mosley Street where we come to the imposing building of the Manchester Central Convention Complex (formerly known as the GMex). Mancunians of a certain age, however, still know it fondly as Manchester Central station.

Manchester Central Station

The station, over the years, was a regular departure point for the travelling United supporters. It was also from here on the afternoon of 25 April 1909 that a triumphant Manchester United team returned from their FA Cup success over Bristol City at Crystal Palace. Thousands gathered on the approach to the station, while countless more waited in nearby Albert Square. Others, wishing to avoid the crush, lined the streets between the two and along the 3-mile route to Clayton. It was later estimated that '100,000, mainly men, but including many women, were out on the streets'. Arriving at the station, the triumphant team were greeted by the band of St Joseph's Industrial School who, as the players appeared, struck up with 'See the Conquering Hero Comes'.

Although the Town Hall was only a short distance from the station, the team and officials travelled in two horse brakes, (belonging to an official of Manchester City no less), with the band in another two, the procession led by mounted police. Charlie Roberts sat proudly at the front, clutching the FA Cup. Every window space along the route was filled and it was commented upon

The victorious 1909 Manchester United FA Cup-winning team depart Manchester Central station on their journey around the city showing off the trophy to their many fans.

A picture of Manchester Central station before it became the G-Mex Exhibition Centre.

that due to the number of workmen present, many must have left their places of employment an hour or two early in order to be there. Having been greeted by the Lord Mayor, it was off to Clayton, not for another knees-up, but for the small matter of an evening fixture against Woolwich Arsenal.

In Oldham Street, shop assistants threw red roses to the players, while in the 'meaner streets of Clayton', the *Manchester Guardian* reported that 'the poorest of the residents had attempted some kind of decoration and the person who moved among the throng without flaunting some red and white ribbon would probably have been thought guilty of heresy'.

Following the ninety minutes against the Londoners, which saw United lose 4-1, it was back to the carriages for the return journey to the city centre and the Midland Hotel for the official club celebrations. Preceded by supporters carrying torches and a band, the procession slowly meandered through the streets, which were once again packed by people, with the journey taking over two hours. Upon arrival at the hotel, there were again large numbers, with the police, mounted and on foot, struggling to keep order.

Due to the time it took to make the 3-mile journey, the seventy people present at the official dinner had their evening cut short due to the lateness of the hour. The party could continue elsewhere, behind closed doors.

The Midland

Retracing our steps back along Mosley Street there is another imposing building, The Midland Hotel, situated on the corner of St Peter Street. The hotel was used regularly by United in the fifties and sixties to host celebration dinners for championship successes, post-match dinners following European fixtures and numerous other occasions.

Before crossing into Albert Square, one United legend could often be seen around St Peter's Square and the site now occupied by the Manchester Central Library, as it was here that Billy Meredith had his sports equipment shop.

In 1906, John Henry Davies, the chairman of Manchester United, provided the funds for Billy Meredith to set up a sports equipment shop, and it was the United winger who provided the distinctive white shirts with red 'V' sashes that United wore in their 1909 FA Cup final victory. Early meetings of the Players' Union were held in a room above the shop. Sadly, later that year, Meredith was forced out of business after a fire on the premises.

The site was cleared in the 1930s to make way for Manchester Central Library and the Town Hall extension.

Above: The Midland Hotel.

Inset: The MUFC Dinner and Dance at the Midland Hotel, 1957.

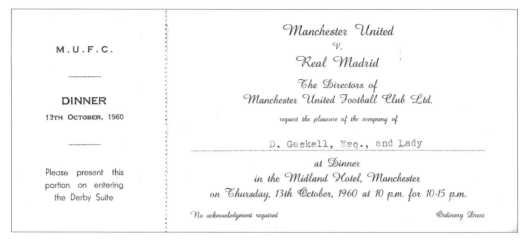

An invite to the MUFC Dinner at the Midland Hotel, 1960.

Albert Square

Like the Midland Hotel, Albert Square has hosted United celebrations, none bigger than when Matt Busby and his players returned home from Wembley in 1968, having beaten Portuguese side Benfica 4-1 to win the European Cup. The United manager stood on the steps of the Town Hall and hoisted the large silver trophy above his head to the acclaim of the thousands thronged in the square.

The Town Hall has also hosted celebration dinners for the club, as well as other lavish functions in honour of United managers Sir Matt Busby and Sir Alex Ferguson, along with Sir Bobby Charlton being awarded the Freedom of the City.

Above: The crowds in Albert Square.

Inset: An invitation to the MUFC Dinner to celebrate winning the FA Challenge Cup, 1948.

New Islington Hall

Elected into Division One when the League was expanded in 1892, Newton Heath struggled in their new environment, finishing bottom in that initial season, five points behind Accrington Stanley, but managing to escape relegation thanks to a 5-2 test match replay victory over Birmingham City at the Victoria Ground, Stoke, following a 1-1 draw at the same venue. Twelve months later, they were once again propping up the table, five points adrift of Darwen, but this time there was no Test Match reprieve, and they lost 2-0 to Liverpool at Ewood Park, Blackburn.

In Division Two, where they were certainly more comfortable, they finished in third place, but still had that outside chance of promotion through the test match system, but lost 3-0 to Stoke City, the third-bottom side in the First Division. Season 1896/97 found the Heathens in second place, three points behind Notts County, once again offering the possibility of promotion via the test Matches, but once again, the opportunity was spurned.

Three consecutive third-place finishes followed, but they suddenly found themselves on a downward slide, finishing tenth and then fifteenth, the latter a mere one point above the relegation zone. Meanwhile, off the field there were concerns about the financial state of the club.

Completely out of the blue, it was reported that the club was faced with a winding up order, mainly due to the fact that a director, Mr W. J. Healey, was owed over £242. On 1 March the Heathen's financial details were made public, while a receiver moved in to try and save the club. At the same time, a number of people showed an interest in purchasing the ground.

Meetings were held, with one reported in the *Manchester Courier and Lancashire General Advertiser* on Wednesday 19 March 1902, under the heading 'Newton Heath Club and its Troubles' as follows:

An Enthusiastic Meeting – What the Chairman described as 'a surprise packet' was sprung upon the crowded meeting of the supporters of the Newton Heath Football Club, held last evening in the New Islington Hall, Ancoats. Elderly men who have followed the fortunes and misfortunes of the 'Heathens' for a quarter of a century, were packed alongside the younger but equally enthusiastic supporters of the club, till there was hardly an inch of standing room left.

To Solve the Problem – Mr F. Palmer was in the chair, and in explaining why a public meeting had not been called at an earlier date, he pointed out that it was not until ten days ago that the executive received the formal sanction of the Football Association to continue to run the club. 'The Association are satisfied' he added with a pardonable touch of pride in his voice, 'that the present directors had nothing to do with the club being landed in the bankruptcy court'. (Cheers.)

After alluding to the loyalty of the players in standing by the directors and being content to let their wages go into arrears, he remarked that the least the supporters of the club could do was to make a strenuous effort to raise the money in order that these arrears be wiped off. (Applause.) They had a good ground – (hear hear) – fairly well equipped, and according to the decision of the Football Association, they would have the option at the end of the season to sign on which players they chose.

The question to be solved was how the club was to be carried on, and it was with the object of arriving at a solution to this question that the meeting had been convened. The present executive could not be expected to run any further risks, observed the Chairman, and the meeting cordially agreed with him. He wisely refrained from going into the details of with regard to the recent winding up of the concern, but gave a gentle hint that if the club was kept on its feet there was a great possibility of their meeting their neighbours from the other side of the city in the Second Division next season – a prospective reminder which elicited loud and prolonged applause.

The Financial Aspect – The Secretary, Mr J. West, enlightened the meeting on the financial side of the club's position. The receipts at the matches played since the winding up order was made amounted to £402 3s 8d and they had paid their debts as they went along week by week with the exception of the player's wages. This item had got behind to the extent of £181 10s 6d. He deplored the bad luck that had persistently dogged the steps of the directors, but concluded by declaring, amidst applause, that there was not the slightest reason why Manchester should not support two of the finest teams in the kingdom.

Mr Smith, one of the oldest directors, and Mr J. Robinson, another enthusiastic member of the executive, gave a full and interesting description of the club's position, and strongly appealed to the supporters to stand by 'the old club'.

A Surprise Packet – It was at this point that the surprise packet was sprung. Mr Harry Stafford, the popular captain of the team, asked the audience what amount would be required to set the club on a sound financial basis, and the Chairman replied that when it was formed into a limited liability company, a sum of £2,000 was asked for, but he did not suppose that the amount would be requisite now, seeing they had a well-equipped ground.

Mr Stafford thereupon stated, to the accompaniment of deafening cheers, that he would give the names of five gentlemen, willing to guarantee £200 each, and pay the money into the bank tomorrow if need be. For two or three minutes, the big audience cheered as only a properly constituted football crowd can cheer,and they would not be content until the captain ascended the platform and told them more about the matter. He said that the names of the individuals were; Mr Davies (Old Trafford), Mr Taylor (Sale), Mr Jones (Manchester), Mr Browne (Denton), and himself. (Cheers.) Then came the question as to whether the new venture would be run as a private club or a limited liability company, and the Secretary and others explained the position from the Football Association's point of view. However, it was of no use discussing the matter till the gentlemen named had met the directors on the subject, and it was eventually decided to adjourn the meeting till this had been done, when another public meeting could be called.

Meantime, one old member suggested changing the name of the club to the Manchester United, and before the crowd dispersed, a number of persons gave their names to the Secretary as willing to take up shares in any new concern that might be formulated.

The Heathens' affairs were now the talk of the city and a public meeting was organised for Thursday 24 April 1902, again at the New Islington public hall and the following day, the *Manchester Courier and Lancashire General Advertiser* reported the following 'Newton Heath FC Club's Name To Be Changed to Manchester United'.

An important public meeting in connection with the Newton Heath Football Club was held in the New Islington Public Hall, Ancoats, Manchester, last evening. The chief business was to consider the future of the club. The hall was packed to utmost capacity, and Mr J. Brown who occupied the chair, said it was intended that Dr Bishop should have presided, but in a letter from that gentleman he stated his business in Parliament prevented him from attending. He, however, expressed himself willing to assist them in placing the old club in the position it once occupied. He hoped, also, the Manchester public would help in giving to Manchester what Manchester should never be without, a first class First League team. (Applause.)

Mr Brown reverted to the fact that he personally, together with Harry Stafford and three others had thought that a thousand pounds would be necessary to lift the club out of the mire. They had offered to find that money, and if the money were to be lost, they were quite content to lose it in the interest of the cause. (Applause.) Further, he wanted them to understand that if the venture was a success the five gentlemen who subscribed the thousand pounds would be willing to draw out their money and turn the whole concern over to a limited company or in any way they thought fit; that was, of course when the club showed signs of making its way. There was no desire whatever on their part to make anything out of the club. They had come forward in a sportsmanlike manner, and having been told, plainly, that Newton Heath as a club was practically defunct, they wanted to give it new lease of life. (Loud and continued applause.)

He wanted them, in conclusion, to take special note that they five, who had promised to subscribe the one thousand pounds, had arranged matters amicably with the old directors. The idea that they were, probably, usurpers was, therefore, out of the question.

Mr West, the secretary of the club, addressed the meeting, and alluded to the action of the gentlemen having subscribed the one thousand pounds in praiseworthy terms. He reminded them that out of that money there were summer wages to be paid, and then again, more important still, there was the strengthening of the team. He, personally, would like to see the whole of the one thousand pounds expended in the latter direction. Season tickets would be printed shortly, and he appealed to supporters to purchase them quickly, in order to assist in the building up of the club.

Harry Stafford, the club's popular player, who is one of the five subscribing the one thousand pounds, said he had done his best in the interest of the club, and if they all would pull in the same direction there was no reason why the club should not be at the top of the Second League next season. During the last fortnight he and others who had the welfare of the club at heart had been round telling the tale to people (the chairman: 'and he can tell the tale, gentlemen') and as a result they have made one hundred pounds, which would be utilised for ground improvements. (Loud cheering.)

The Change of the Club's Name – The chairman then brought the most important proposition of the evening forward, the one of changing the club's name. It had been mentioned to him that during the season one or two visiting clubs had been deluded by the name of the club in taking the wrong car, through being mistaken as to the situation of the ground. In consequence delay in commencement of a number of matches had been entailed. On this ground, and other of even a stronger character, he would suggest that the club's name should be changed, on the approval of the League and the Football Association, to that of Manchester United. Whatever, at any rate, their decision would be, he would strongly urge that the word Manchester should be associated with it in some way.

The question was asked, would the new club be likely to be readmitted to the Second Division under the name of Manchester United?

In this photograph from the early 1900s New Islington Hall is on the left, next to the baths and public washhouse. The hall part of the building was demolished by the 1960s, but the baths survived for several years longer.

In reply, Mr West (the secretary) said they would have to make application to the League for permission to change the name, but he anticipated there would be no difficulty in obtaining the necessary consent. The club had supporters from all parts of the city, and that being the case justification in changing the name was warranted. He admitted they got the bulk of the Newton Heath supporters, and if the name of Newton Heath could be retained without any disadvantage to the club he would prefer it. It would not be of benefit, however, to keep the old name, and he really thought the word Manchester should be associated with it.

The matter was eventually put to the vote, and by a vast majority it was agreed to change the name of the club from Newton Heath to that of Manchester United, providing that the League and Football Association were in approval thereof. It was resolved to elect a working men's committee of fifteen to assist the new directors in the management of the club.

The name, however, was accepted and approved by the Football League and on 6 September 1902 at Gainsborough Trinity, Manchester United took the field for the first time, celebrating with a 1-0 victory.

How to find the site where the New Islington Hall once stood: turning left off Oldham Road, you find yourself in Great Ancoats Street. Taking the third turning on the left is Redhill Street, which turns into New Union Street and then, briefly, New Islington before turning into Weybridge Road. It's on the New Islington Stretch, across from the new houses called Islington Square, that the hall once stood. At the time of writing, the site is under redevelopment.

The Queens Hotel, Piccadilly

Continuing down Weybridge Street and turning right onto Old Mill Street, continue across Great Ancoats Street and into Store Street, turning right into Piccadilly.

On the corner opposite Newton Street stood the Queens Hotel, and it was here in December 1906 where the final details of the transfers of Manchester City players Herbert Burgess, Sandy Turnbull and Jimmy Bannister were finalised by manager Ernest Mangnall. After the turn of that century, and after Newton Heath had changed its name to Manchester United, from a general player's point of view there was a lot of unrest regarding the pay that they were receiving from their clubs. Most top players were earning no more than £3–4 per week in the playing season, and only £2 per week during the summer close season. This was despite playing in front of large crowds, some in excess of 35,000. Obviously the players were not happy and started agitating for a bigger wage because of the revenues that their play was generating. The clubs were then rumoured to be paying players 'under-the-counter payments' and it was no real surprise when, in 1905, the Football Association began an investigation.

Several clubs came under close scrutiny including Manchester United but, fortunately for them, there were no findings of any impropriety. Their neighbours across the city though were less fortunate, with the Consultative Committee at the Football Association finding Manchester City guilty of not only making illegal payments to their players, but also making illegal payments in their transfer dealings. In May 1906, with several of their directors having been suspended for a number of years, even more trouble surfaced for City when they were once again found to be paying players illegal payments, and seventeen players were suspended for six months and banned from ever playing for City again.

The City directors put the players up for sale and notified the other League clubs that there would be an auction for the players' registrations, although there had been considerable activity at City's Hyde Road ground in the build-up to the auction that was to be held at the Queen's Hotel in December 1906. On the night of the auction, as officials, secretaries, and managers of other clubs took their seats in one of the hotel's lounges, Ernest Magnall the Manchester United manager was seen to appear out of a room adjoining the lounge. What those other club representatives did not know was that a few days prior to the auction date, Magnall had been in touch with Manchester City and had obtained permission to speak to several of the City players who he wanted to sign before the auction began. Magnall signed the best of the players who were up for sale and, as he walked out of the lounge before the auction began, he had in his possession signed contracts for Turnbull, Burgess and Bannister. These three players were to play a part in the rise to the first major successes that Manchester United ever achieved – the First Division championship in 1908 and 1911, and the FA Cup win in 1909. Billy Meredith had already agreed to join United for free, having felt that it would be wrong to pay any fee for him. The City management were far from pleased.

The Queen's Hotel in later years, especially after the Second World War, became the hotel that most clubs from the South of England and the Midlands preferred to stay at when they faced opposition in the North West. At various times Lancashire in particular boasted as many as nine clubs in the top echelon, and their home stadia were all in easy reach of the Queen's Hotel. On

Friday evenings and Saturday mornings throughout the football season, there would be many young autograph hunters stood on the steps of the hotel waiting to capture the signatures of some of the most well-known stars that were playing football in Britain at that time.

The hotel, however, was at one time the Manchester home of William Houldsworth, who was born in 1771 at Hagg Farm, Gonalston, a small village to the south of Lowdham in Nottinghamshire. Apprenticed to a stocking weaver in his early years, he learned his trade in the cotton industry and in 1793, together with his brothers, they started a cotton spinning business in Manchester. They soon became entrepreneurs, and branched out their business to Rocester in Staffordshire, Pontefract in Yorkshire, and Glasgow in Scotland, a move that brought the brothers considerable wealth.

Much of William Houldsworth's time was spent in Manchester overseeing his business interests, so he decided to build a home upon the site of a bowling green that was situated on the corner of what is now known as Piccadilly and Portland Street, but back then was known as Portland Place. Upon his death, he bequeathed the Manchester home to his nephew Thomas, who in 1845 turned the house into a hotel. Thomas was another well-known Manchester cotton merchant who had his premises in Lever Street very close to the new hotel. He was a man who was very popular with all classes of society and particularly with his employees.

In Portland Place, the other two houses were owned by a cotton spinner named Robert Ogden, and two business partners named Hargreaves and Dugdale, who were calico printers and had their premises in Marsden's Square close by. Houldsworth was able to persuade the other two homeowners to sell their properties to him. These buildings were added to transform the hotel into a much bigger going concern. This became the original Queen's Hotel. The hotel, with over 100 bedrooms, built up a fine reputation for its furnishings and fittings, and comfort and service. Before the turn of the nineteenth century the hotel had played host to, among others, the kings of Belgium, Portugal and Romania, the Emperor of Brazil, Prince Napoleon, President Grant, General Gordon of Khartoum, Charles Dickens, and William Makepeace Thackeray. It had a worldwide reputation.

The Queens Hotel also had the reputation for being the finest hotel in the city and survived the war, but no longer stands, having been replaced by what is today known as No. 1 Portland Street by Charles White and William Hood in 1974.

St Cross Church

From here, we now continue south, turning left onto Old Mill Street, before taking the first right onto Carruthers Street, before joining the A662, turning left onto Merill Street, which becomes Ashton New Road. Continuing along this, we pass the Etihad Stadium on the left and shortly after crossing Alan Turing Way you will come to Clayton Park on your left, where you will find St Cross church (611 Ashton New Road, M11 4UA). Here, you will find the resting place of United's legendary captain Charlie Roberts.

Charles 'Charlie' Roberts is written into the folklore of the Manchester United Football Club. He captained the club during those golden years in the decade just after the turn of the twentieth century when the club had its first tangible successes. Born in Rise Carr just north of Darlington, County Durham, on 6 April 1883, Roberts was one of the first football stars to come out of an area that throughout the history of the football game has produced many splendid players. He worked as an iron-furnace worker, playing football as an amateur for the famous Bishop

CHURCHMAN'S CIGARETTES.

C . ROBERTS.

Charlie Roberts.

Auckland. Tall and good-looking, Roberts had an outstanding physique standing over 6 feet tall and weighing over 13 stone. Broad shouldered, he was built with all the physical attributes that go into making a good commanding centre-half.

In the summer of 1903, when he was just twenty years old, he signed professional forms for Grimsby Town. On 26 April 1904, after playing just thirty-one games for the 'Fishermen', Ernest Magnall, the Manchester United secretary-manager, took Roberts to Old Trafford, paying Grimsby Town what was then a huge record sum of £600 in a transfer fee. So began what was to prove a glorious association that lasted for over nine years and saw the club through its first halcyon years of success.

Roberts was appointed club captain at the start of the 1904/05 season and it was a position he was to hold until he left the club in 1913. Like many United players after him, Roberts had his first brush with the FA that season, and he was cited for wearing his football shorts too high above the knee. The FA passed a law stipulating that shorts should be worn below the knees – but they never had any success in enforcing the rule as most players in the League completely ignored it.

Leading by example, Roberts was tall, quick, strong in the tackle, excellent in the air, and a tremendous passer of the ball, and although he was the lynchpin and pivot of the team, he was certainly not what could have been termed as 'the normal centre-half'. He put his brains where others put their bodies in a game where physical strength counted for too much. His game was based on interception and creativity, and there is little doubt that he was the first centre-half to play the game in this fashion. It was no surprise then that he caught the eye of the England selectors and was selected for the national team on three occasions during that year. Sadly, these were to be the only three caps that he was ever to win.

In April 1907, Tommy Blackstock, a colleague at Manchester United, collapsed after heading a ball during a reserve game against St Helens and sadly, the twenty-five-year-old died soon afterwards. An inquest into his death returned a verdict of 'Natural Causes' and once again a football player's family received no compensation. Roberts was appalled by the way Blackstock's family was treated and joined up with colleagues, Billy Meredith, Charlie Sagar, Herbert Burgess, and Sandy Turnbull, to form a new Players' Union. It was probably because of his Union activities that Roberts was

Above left: An advert for Charlie Roberts' tobacconist at 591 Ashton New Road, Clayton.

Above right: The Outcasts FC.

never selected to play for England again, although he did play nine times for the Football League. Just before the start of the 1909 cup final at Crystal Palace, the FA Secretary, Sir Frederick Wall, visited the Manchester United dressing room. Roberts asked him to leave in no uncertain fashion as he, as captain, wanted to have some last private words with his team before they went out to face Bristol City. Wall was almost apoplectic at what he considered to be Roberts' insolence.

Just after United's FA Cup victory over Bristol City, the FA, the Football League, and the Player's Union were all at loggerheads. Roberts and Billy Meredith were prime movers in the reorganisation of the Union and for its affiliation with the General Federation of Trade Unions (GFTU). The FA and the League felt themselves threatened and that the football programme could be easily shut down by the GFTU due to any of its other bodies going on strike. The FA reacted quickly and immediately withdrew its recognition of the Union. It also ordered that all of the Union members should resign from the Union or their player registrations would be cancelled.

The Union (led by Roberts and Meredith and chaired by J. T. Jones of the Municipal Employer's Association) called a meeting at the Albion Hotel in Piccadilly, Manchester (which later became the Woolworths building on the corner of Oldham Street and Piccadilly), to which 200 players turned up, and the two United players were able to get their members to stand firm. In his memoirs, Roberts was to write:

I refused to resign from the Union. At the next meeting of the FA the whole of the Manchester United players were suspended. That meeting was held on a Saturday morning and I remember the day very well. I am a newsagent in Manchester and when the evening newspapers arrived the posters read 'Manchester United without a Team'.

During the summer months of 1909, interest focused on the United players who met with other players at the Fallowfield Stadium and carried on training. They formed a team named 'The Outcasts' and it was Charlie Roberts who came up with that name.

After training one day, a photographer came along to take a photo of us and we willingly obliged him. While the boys were being arranged I obtained a piece of wood and wrote on it

'The Outcasts Football Club 1909' and sat down with it in front of me to be photographed. The next day, that photograph of the Outcasts FC (showing the board and all the players) had the front page of a newspaper much to our enjoyment and the disgust of our opponents.

With the start of the 1909/10 season drawing ever closer, it was clear that the players were going to strike and it looked as though the season would not get under way on the scheduled date. There was an initial meeting between the FA and the Union executive to talk things over. In late August both parties came to an agreement on Union recognition and questions related to legal cases, but an overall settlement foundered on the FA's refusal to accept the Union demands that the Manchester United players receive their outstanding summer pay.

The season started as it was scheduled to, and the Manchester United players ran out for the first game at home to Bradford City wearing their Players' Union armbands. Within a month, the Football League banned their armbands. Their summer back pay would take over six months to be paid, and Roberts' benefit match against Newcastle United was refused. Within three months, after relentless pressure from both the League and the FA, the FA got its way when at a Union meeting it was decided to hold a ballot of all members to decide whether to remain affiliated to the GFTU. The vote was decisively against by 470:172. Roberts was bitterly disappointed. He went on to say:

I know of no class of work-people who are less able to look after themselves than footballers. They are like a lot of sheep. But I am telling you now that I have just about had enough of trying to raise the status of the professional footballer. It takes up time that I am unable to spare … He is a wretched miserable fool who cannot see what is good for himself.

Roberts still slogged on for the cause though, and in 1913, after playing some 271 games for Manchester United and scoring twenty-two goals, he moved on to Oldham Athletic. He was

The tombstone of former United skipper
Charlie Roberts, who lies at rest in
St Cross church, Clayton, Manchester.

told by the club, 'We have agreed to transfer you to Oldham Athletic, subject, of course, to your consent for the sum of £1500.' Charlie wrote, 'Fancy, the United almost ten years before had paid Grimsby Town £600 for me, and now they wanted a profit of £900 on me before I could get another situation, and yet we sing, "Britons Never Will Be Slaves".'

The Cliff, Lower Broughton

Leaving the resting place of Charlie Roberts, turn left onto the A6010, then right onto the Ashton Old Road (A635), joining the Mancunian Way – A57. You then want the A56 – Bury, which takes you through the city centre, along Deansgate and onto Bury New Road. Watch for signs for the A576, turning left, before turning right into Lower Broughton Road. The Cliff (M7 2HU) is on the left, just past Hugh Oldham Drive.

Situated in Lower Broughton, The Cliff was the home of Broughton Rangers Rugby League club from 1913 to 1933, but was taken over by Manchester United in June 1938 and used as a training ground and for practice matches for the club's junior sides. It was purchased outright by the club in 1951, floodlights were installed and it became something of a home ground to United's youth team, hosting many of their early FA Youth Cup ties.

In those immediate post-war years, United's first-team players would train at Old Trafford; however, due to wear and tear on the pitch, training was switched on a permanent basis to The Cliff, making it the destination of countless autograph hunters and those simply wishing to see their idols up close. The players of the now distant past were much more accommodating than those of today.

As the 1990s approached, it was decided that United had by now outgrown those somewhat spartan surroundings, with the increasing number of daily 'visitors' and media interest forcing the management into looking for more private facilities and a new training facility was built at Carrington. The Cliff, however, remained, with the younger members of the club's personnel still using it to hone their skills, watched over by the ghosts of the likes of Duncan Edwards, Eddie Colman and David Pegg.

The Cliff training ground.

Manchester Amateur League
1903 — JUBILEE YEAR — 1953

Manchester United XI.
versus
M/c. Amateur League
at The Cliff, Broughton,
on Wednesday Night, March 11th.

Kick-off 7-0 p.m.   Admission 1/-

7-15

Above: A ticket to the Manchester United *v.* M/C Amateur League at The Cliff, Broughton, 1953.

Below: The programme for the floodlit Manchester United XI *v.* Northern Nomads friendly match, 1952.

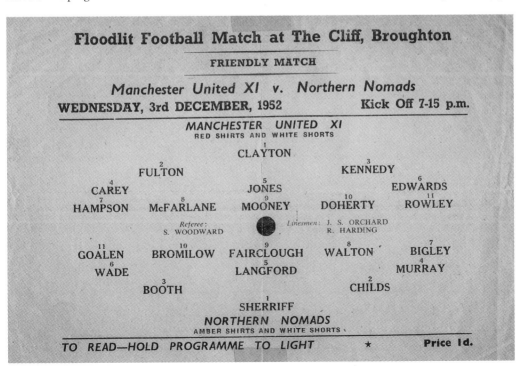

Floodlit Football Match at The Cliff, Broughton

FRIENDLY MATCH

Manchester United XI v. Northern Nomads
WEDNESDAY, 3rd DECEMBER, 1952   Kick Off 7-15 p.m.

MANCHESTER UNITED XI
RED SHIRTS AND WHITE SHORTS

1
CLAYTON

2   3
FULTON   KENNEDY

4   5   6
CAREY   JONES   EDWARDS

7   8   9   10   11
HAMPSON   McFARLANE   MOONEY   DOHERTY   ROWLEY

Referee: *Linesmen:* J. S. ORCHARD
S. WOODWARD   R. HARDING

11   10   9   8   7
GOALEN   BROMILOW   FAIRCLOUGH   WALTON   BIGLEY

6   5   4
WADE   LANGFORD   MURRAY

3   2
BOOTH   CHILDS

1
SHERRIFF

NORTHERN NOMADS
AMBER SHIRTS AND WHITE SHORTS

TO READ—HOLD PROGRAMME TO LIGHT   ★   Price 1d.

St John's Church, Pendlebury

Leaving the resting place of Charlie Roberts, turn left onto the A6010, then right onto the Ashton New Road (A635), joining the Mancunian Way and then the A57 – Regents Road, heading west past the Ordsall estate, an area we will revisit shortly and follow.

At the roundabout, take the A6 exit and signs for M60/A666 and follow the road to the junction of A6/A580/A666, taking the third exit on the roundabout onto Bolton Road (A666) and immediately on the right, is St John the Evangelist Church (M27 8XR), the resting place of Geoff Bent, perhaps the lesser known of all those United players who died in the Munich air disaster on 6 February 1958.

Bent was a local lad, born in Salford on 27 September 1932 and attended St John's Junior school, where he won a scholarship for Tootal Grammar.

A member of the Boys Brigade, Geoff was a keen sportsman and although his father was an enthusiastic rugby man, it was football and swimming that the youngster enjoyed most. Strangely, it was in the latter of his two leisure activities that he was awarded his first medal, after rescuing a youngster from drowning in the Salford Canal. During his early footballing days he occupied the old inside-left position, later moving back to left-half. Such were his performances at schoolboy level, he not simply represented Salford Boys in the England Schools Trophy of 1947, but captained the side.

His performances caught the eye of numerous clubs, but it was his mother who played a major part in the fifteen-year-old signing for United, as she did not want her only child moving away from home, telling him to sign for a local club.

At Old Trafford, Geoff made his final positional switch, to left-back, and progressed through the junior ranks, while also serving his apprenticeship as a junior alongside another United youngster by the name of Duncan Edwards. A regular place in the Central League side was soon claimed, but his progress was now halted, as the man holding down the first-team left-back spot was England international Roger Byrne. Geoff, however, was more than content to bide his time and on 11 December 1954 he finally made his first-team debut at Turf Moor Burnley, a game that United won 4-2.

Despite the lack of opportunities and the knowledge that he could command a regular starting place in almost any other side in the country, he remained loyal to United, and by February 1958 he had only accumulated a dozen first-team appearances, supplementing his meagre first-team wages with summer employment as a joiner. An injury to Roger Byrne prior to the trip to Belgrade put the United captain's starting place in some doubt, so Geoff made the fateful trip in his role as stand-in. It was a journey that was to cost him his life.

On the Monday evening following the crash in Munich, the bodies of those killed arrived back in Britain and Geoff's, along with most of his teammates', made the solemn journey from Ringway Airport to Old Trafford, where the bodies lay for the night in the club gymnasium. The following morning, it left for St John's church, (where he had been christened and married) with the funeral service held on Tuesday 13 February.

Above: The grave of Geoff Bent, St John's church, Pendlebury.

Right: Geoff Bent in action.

Far right: St John's church, Pendlebury.

Weaste Cemetery/Ordsall, Salford

Retracing our route, we head back down the A6 (Broad Street) and the A5063 (Albion Way) and at the roundabout take the third exit onto the A57, Eccles New Road, carrying on for a few hundred yards before turning left into Cemetery Road, just past the tram stop (M5 5NR). This takes us up to the gates of Weaste Cemetery, resting place of local boy Eddie Colman.

The diminutive wing-half was born at No. 9 Archie Street, Ordsall, a short walk from the cemetery and an even shorter walk from where he plied his trade as a footballer at Old Trafford. Eddie first caught the eye of Matt Busby and his able assistant Jimmy Murphy during a Salford and Stockport schoolboy fixture at United's The Cliff training ground, a sighting that the United management team noted and filed. Upon leaving school in 1952, the youngster was somewhat shocked to find the United manager on his doorstep wanting to sign him.

Above left: Eddie Colman.

Above middle: The grave of Eddie Colman.

Above right: The statue from Eddie Colman's grave.

An able cricketer and basketball player (despite his size), it was with a football at his feet that he excelled, and in the all-conquering United Youth side, his talents were soon seized upon by an even wider audience.

Despite the volume of exceptional players in that United youth team – David Pegg, Albert Scanlon, John Doherty and a certain Duncan Edwards – Eddie Colman still stood out, and following steady progress through the juniors and the Central League side, he was rewarded with his first-team debut on 12 November 1955 at Burnden Park, Bolton, eleven days after his nineteenth birthday.

It was only a matter of time before the name of Eddie Colman was a regular feature on the United first eleven team sheet as his natural talent began to blossom through, while his background ensured that he was physically strong enough to compete at the highest level. His ability to send an opponent the wrong way with a simple shake of his hips captured the imagination of the supporters and also the national press.

His only failure was his timekeeping for training, as despite living closer to the ground than most, he was constantly late, leaving Jimmy Murphy to query whether or not the swing bridge on Trafford Road had turned to allow a ship to pass through!

By 1958, Eddie was on the verge of full England international honours, but they were never to come his way, as along with many of his teammates, he was to perish in the Munich air disaster. The statuette shown above at one time stood to the left-hand side of Eddie's grave, but was removed by his father following constant vandalism.

To find Eddie's grave, simply follow the path from the gates and when you reach a small roundabout, the grave is beside the path on the right.

Leaving Weaste Cemetery we turn right, back onto Eccles New Road, and at the roundabout we take the A5063 onto Trafford Road, heading towards Old Trafford. At the traffic lights, where there is a right turning towards Salford Quays and on the left a Tesco Express, this was the corner of Archie Street, home to the Colman family and countless others. It was also the street upon which *Coronation Street* was modelled for the on-running television soap opera.

The frontage of the former White
City Stadium.

From Archie Street, we retrace the steps that Eddie Colman would have taken as he walked to
Old Trafford, but instead of turning right once across the Trafford Road swing bridge, follow the
signs for Altrincham, which takes you onto the A56 Chester Road. Turning onto Chester Road,
you will notice an imposing white gateway on your left (a Grade II listed building), situated in
front of a retail park. This was the former White City Stadium.

Built in 1827, on land belonging to the de Trafford family, it was the entrance into what were
the Botanical Gardens. Later it was to become the White City Amusement Park, which was
opened in 1907 and between 1928 and 1981 it was also known as the White City Greyhound
Stadium, before finally closing. In the immediate aftermath of the Munich air disaster, United
held training sessions here, using jumpers and suchlike for goalposts, with the players walking
the short distance from Old Trafford.

Old Trafford

Match day at Old Trafford today is a vastly different experience than that of three or four
decades ago, when the terraces swayed with the flow of the game, anthems echoing around
the ground. There was also no sauntering towards the turnstiles five or ten minutes prior
to kick-off, as you often had to ensure you were inside the ground an hour before kick-off
to ensure your place on the terracing and not be left outside the ground with the red gates
firmly locked in front of you.

Some of the approach roads resemble an Eastern market, while the accents heard around the
ground come from the four corners of the world – such is the global appeal of the club. Many of
those who click through the turnstiles are unaware of the history of either the club or indeed the
ground. Others, however, have not simply witnessed all the notable players throughout the years,
but also watched transfixed as the ground itself took on an entirely different look.

Although J. H. Davies had helped get the club back on its feet in 1902 with his financial backing,
thus enabling the supporters to enjoy First Division football again following a twelve-year spell
in the Second Division (having gained promotion at the end of season 1905/06), he was very
concerned about the conditions at Clayton. He thought that they were an embarrassment to the
club and not ideal for playing top class football.

Nor were they ideal for a club who wanted to play its football in the top flight, even though a representative match between the Football League and their Scottish counterparts had been played there on 4 April 1904. John Davies was not a man to rush into things and he certainly did not squander his money or invest it in projects where there was little or no return. But he had set his sights on finding a new home for his football team and he scoured the city for a new site worthy of his beloved United, before deciding upon a spot to the south-west of the city centre, alongside the Bridgewater Canal at Old Trafford.

Stories relate that the money to purchase the ground came from the Brewery Company, owned by Davies, but the site was actually purchased by the United chairman himself, with the money for its purchase coming from the sale of the Holford Hall estate at Lostock Gralam near Northwich. A property he had purchased for £3,000 and had sold to the ICI for £72,000 after he discovered salt on the land. When the cheque arrived, he declared, 'The Manchester working man is going to have the best football team and ground that can be had.' 'Mancunian' of the *Cricket and Football Field* did not share the chairman's opinion regarding the proposed new home for Manchester United, writing:

> I consider it too far from the centre of the city. Nor do I think it would be fair to the present supporters, who have stuck to the club through adversity, to take another ground on the opposite side of the city to that from which they have always drawn their patronage, for I don't think they would follow them.

How wrong he was to be, not only in the near but also distant future.

In the *Athletic News* dated 8 March 1909 an article entitled 'A Pen Picture Of The Undertaking' by a correspondent called 'Tityrus' described the proposed move to pastures new in great detail and even today it makes very interesting reading:

> The west of Manchester is destined to be the Mecca of sportsmen of that great commercial city. 'To the west, to the west' will be the cry of our football folks when leaves are falling next autumn. Already we have the Lancashire County Cricket ground, the polo ground, the curling pond, the Manchester Gun Club and numerous other organisations of similar character, devoted to pastime and recreation to the west of the city.
>
> In September, the Manchester United Football Club will fling open its portals and bid all welcome in the same locality. The contrast between Clayton and the new headquarters of this great football club need not be insisted upon. Clayton is situated in the very heart of the working class community, and dominated on every hand by bout forty huge stacks of chimneys belching forth ciminerion smoke and malodorous fumes. No doubt there are those who feel thankful for a football ground in the vicinity, as it does tend to remind the immediate residents that there is some space left where the toiling people can be amused in a healthy and vigorous manner that pleases them. But an ambitious and a vast club like Manchester United appeals to the 800,000 folks of Manchester and Salford, and an area of larger dimensions, with better accommodation for seeing and housing the spectators and situated in a more attractive locality became essential. Hence the decision of the enterprising directors to lay out an enclosure in the west of Manchester.
>
> The new ground lies between the Cheshire Lines Railway and the Bridgewater Canal, being a little to the left of the Warwick Road North which juts off the Cheshire Road. In other words, walking along the Chester Road towards Stretford, one would turn to

the south along Warwick Road for the County cricket ground and exactly opposite to the north for Manchester United football ground.

The goals in the new arena will be almost west and east, the Stretford goal being the west and the Old Trafford goal to the east. This will give the readers an idea of the exact environment in the locality that is expanding. There will not be any difficulty in reaching the new rendezvous. Electric tramcars already run from Clayton to Old Trafford and from the city direct, by two routes. It is proposed to lay down a circular tramway siding just off Chester Road so that cars can be turned in there, and the passengers having disembarked, the cars can run round the western end of the circle and return to Manchester for more freight.

There is here a bridge over the Cheshire Lines Railway that is to be widened so as to cope with the traffic, while further north on the other side of the ground it is intended to throw a bridge over the canal. But apart from those approaches we understand that the Cheshire Lines committee will open a special station within two or three minutes' walk of the western end of this home of sport, so that people can step off the train into the immediate precincts. With such conveniences as these there should never be any difficulty in getting to the place or away from it.

The Manchester United club have resolved to lay out and equip a huge ground wholly and solely dedicated to football. There will be a running or cycling track around the grass, and for football alone there will be no better enclosure in England. It is to accommodate 100,000 people and if the greatest matches of the day are not in turn decided to Manchester we shall be surprised, especially as the club is not frightened to expend £30,000 on the undertaking.

When sightseers cross over the railway bridge, they will find themselves in the midst of a clear space which will serve as a gathering ground for 120 feet broad for spectators and the need not be congestion in gaining access to any portion. With this ground laid out for football alone, the sightseers are brought as near as possible to the playing portion.

The ground will be rectangle in shape with the corners rounded and it is designed so that everybody will be able to see. The pitch for the game will be excavated to a depth of nine feet from the ground level so that the boundary or containing wall that is to surround the whole place will only be 30 feet high. There are numerous and spacious exits round the ground. Ingress will be easy and it is estimated that a full ground can be emptied in five minutes.

Now let us assume that the ordinary spectator has passed through the turnstile. He will find himself in a passage twenty feet broad, which girdles the whole area. From this, access can be obtained from any portion of the popular terracing, which is virtually divided into three sections. There will be one hundred steps of terracing constructed on a special plan and a nicely judged gradient with of course Leitch's patient crush barriers. The lower portion of this terracing is solid ground; the next higher is formed by the excavated earth and the last and highest is built entirely of ferro-concrete, which is as hard as rock and non-flammable.

With his practical experience of all the best grounds in these islands, Mr Archibald Leitch MIME of Manchester, who has been the only designer, has endeavoured to cope with these problems. There seems every reason to believe that he has solved it. Now, from this twenty foot passage which will of course afford protection from rain until it absolutely necessary to go into the arena, the herds of human beings can melt away at will. Right in front of the visitor, whichever entrance they take, will be a flight of very broad but easy stairs, which end in a wide opening or mouth, 60 feet wide and split into three sections.

The stream of sightseers mounting these stairs and reaching the opening find themselves rather above the middle of the terracing which they can spread themselves at will. We can picture these great mouths vomiting thousands upon thousands human beings onto this glorious amphitheatre. The advantage of each mouth is its central position. But if the spectator wishes to go right on top of the terracing, any tier above sixteenth, he will take another wide staircase which hugs the inside of the boundary wall and lands him an the top of forty tiers of concrete, resting on foundations of the same material, the space underneath being utilised for refreshment rooms and other conveniences.

Means are provided for transferring from one portion of the ground to another, but it is expected that in a ground devised on this plan, with so many conveniences for reaching the particular position that the spectator desires, there will be little call for transfers and certainly not to the same extent as on other enclosures.

The accommodation will, as said, provide for 100,000 people. Of these, 12,000 will be seated in the grandstand and 24,000 standing under steel and slated roofs, so that together there will be room for 36,000 folk under cover and 64,000 in the open, divided between the two arcs of a circle and the mammoth terracing behind each goal. The roofed part for the populace will be on the southern side and will have wide open ends with overhanging eaves so that no portion of this erection will obstruct the view of those who are not fortunate enough to secure its shelter on an inclement day.

The special feature of the grandstand compared with similar erections is that there will not be a paddock in front of it. The spectators will be seated from the barricade round the pitch direct to the back of the stand, in fifty tiers. These fifty tiers are again divided into three sections, the lower, the middle and the highest. Spectators desiring to be comfortable in the grandstand will enter from the turnstiles facing the mouth of Chester Road. They are especially reserved for grandstand visitors only and there they can only obtain tickets for any part of the stand.

Entering there, the spectators will find themselves in a corridor along which run tea-rooms, referee apartments, the player's facilities, a gym, billiard room and laundry. All of which are to be fitted up in the most modern manner. From this central corridor, there are means of access to three sections of the grandstand. The lowest or front portion will be approached by a number of passages on the ground floor. To the middle or central portion there are stairs that run practically the whole length of the stand. The highest part is to be gained by means of a distributing passage that is as long as the stand and 20 feet broad. Stairs lead from this to the loftiest section. Thus it will be seen that the structure is designed in such a manner that each person will be able to get to his seat with the least discomfort to himself and the minimum inconvenience to his neighbours, because there is a separate means of ingress to each section of the stand.

The man who wishes to go to the top of the stand has not to disturb those sitting in the lower rungs and this applies to each portion for every detail has been carefully thought out, both by Mr Leitch the mastermind and Messers Bramfield and Smith of Manchester who were responsible for the extensions and improvements at the Clayton ground, the present home of Manchester United FC.

Altogether, the entire area of the new home of Manchester United will be 16 acres. The outward circumference of the ground will be about 2,000 feet. The ground will be 630 feet long and 510 feet broad, with the width of the terracing being 120 feet. This is a palatial

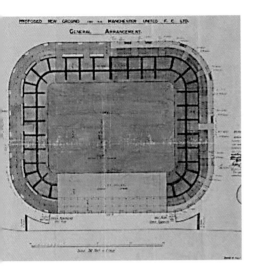

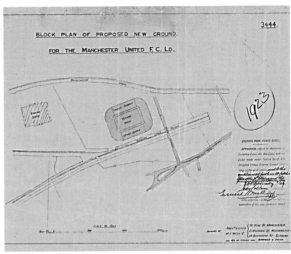

Above left: A complete plan of the ground, showing the whole stadium.

Above right: A block plan of the proposed new ground for Manchester United at Trafford Park, 1923.

Right: Detail of the Grand Stand.

Below: Detail of the elevations.

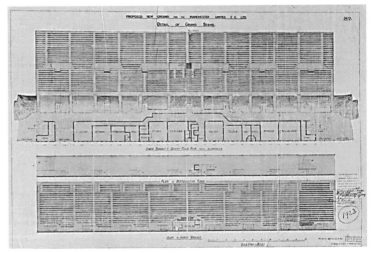

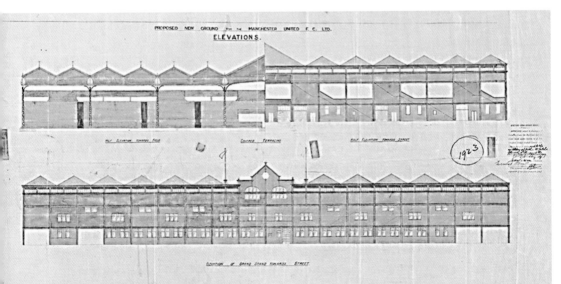

Site of the proposed football ground at Trafford Park.

ground that will challenge comparison with any in Great Britain. The executives of the club are to be congratulated on their spirited policy that no doubt will be met with reward from the football public.

For those familiar with the ground up until the early sixties, it is not difficult to visualise those vivid plans for the stadium from those bygone days. However, before finalising the plans, Mr J. J. Bentley, the club secretary, suggested several refinements, such as the cycle track, reducing the height of the terracing and omitting the cover on the terracing opposite the Main Stand. The latter of course meant a reduction in the planned 100,000 capacity by around 20,000, but the original plans were felt perhaps to be just a little too ambitious and this reduction did in fact cut the costs of the project to around £60,000, which was also something of a deciding factor, even though the final figure was twice the sum first reported as the cost of the new stadium.

In an effort to make an indent in the final cost of the new stadium, no matter how small, Archibald Leitch did try to involve the Cheshire Lines Railway in the project. From his Manchester office at No. 78 King Street, he contacted James Pinion, the manager of the Railway Committee and a letter from Leitch, on 27 May 1908, set out his ideas and proposals. It read:

In reference to my interview with you, I shall be glad to know whether your Committee would be willing to entertain a proposal to loan the Manchester United Club the sum of £10,000 for the purpose of erecting the Grand Stand at the NEW Football Ground.

The Club Directors would be willing to give their personal guarantees and also a guarantee from the Club itself; in addition a guarantee would be obtained from the Manchester Brewery Co. and Messrs Walker and Humphreys, Brewers in both of which Companies Mr Davies, chairman of the Manchester United Football Club, is also chairman. The money would be repayable say in five years at a rate of £2,000 yearly, or it might be arranged that half of the net drawings of the grandstand taken yearly would go towards the reduction of the debt. In this way the money might be refunded at an earlier date, but without going further into details at the present moment I shall be glad to know whether your Committee as already stated are willing to entertain this proposal.

Three days after receiving the letter, James Pinion sent a memorandum to all the other committee members outlining the proposal, while also mentioning the construction of a station, something that was not mentioned in the original letter, but something that must have been brought up by Archibald Leitch at his earlier meeting with James Pinion. The memorandum, entitled 'Manchester United Football Club, proposed new Ground in Trafford Park immediately alongside the Cheshire Line Railway' read as follows:

The estimated cost of this ground with stands and other accommodation is £60,000. The estimated cost of the station shewn (*sic*) on the plan prepared by Mr Blundell for the accommodation of traffic to and from is £10,000. The ground is to be constructed so as to accommodate 100,000 spectators. The football season extends over a period of thirty-three weeks and estimating that on twenty Saturdays during the season, matches will be held on the ground and that we obtain the carrying of one-tenth of the number the ground is estimated to accommodate, it would mean the conveyance of 10,000 per match on twenty Saturdays, bringing up an aggregate of 200,000 from Manchester during the season.

In addition, on the remaining twenty Saturdays comprising the year it is proposed to hold athletic meetings, cycling meetings and such like and that we shall have 1,000 on each such Saturday, making up a total of 20,000 for athletic gatherings or 220,000 passengers altogether in the year.

In addition to this estimate for the Manchester traffic there is to be reckoned traffic from Liverpool, Warrington and other stations on the Cheshire Lines proper and also traffic from such places as Derby, Sheffield, Nottingham etc, on the Parent Companies Lines and a great many other places on foreign lines, but reckoning the passenger traffic alone from Manchester the proposal appears to be an enticing one from a Cheshire lines point of view.

I should state that it is the intention of the Football Club to provide elaborate provision for substantial refreshments for large parties coming from a distance so that footballers coming from such remote places as Derby, Sheffield, Nottingham etc., will on arrival on the ground obtain liquid refreshment and refreshments of a more substantial character so that it appears to me the proposal is one to be viewed with considerable favour.

I may mention that such a station as is proposed, with the White city less than half a mile distant and Old Trafford Cricket Ground just half a mile away, would suit admirably for both these places so that the proposal has not alone the football Company's clientele to cater for but also the possibility of a very large traffic for the White City and for the Cricket matches at Old Trafford.

Above and left: Two photographs of work being carried out on the Old Trafford site.

Despite James Pinion obviously being enthusiastic about the proposal, with the idea of the three old pennies fare possibly generating around an extra £2,750 per annum a particularly appealing and a fair return for the initial £9,800 outlay, a preliminary meeting of the committee, held on 1 June, thought otherwise. From the minutes of that meeting came the following:

> The Committee regret exceedingly their statuary powers do not permit of them lending money for such purposes otherwise the Manchester United Company's proposal would have every consideration. With regard to the erection of a station adjoining the football ground it was agreed to defer the consideration of this until the next meeting of the general Managers when Manager proposes to put further information before them.

Various letters and copies of the plans passed to and fro, but in the end, the original plans came to nothing, although a station was later built slightly further down the line, at Trafford Bar.

The plans for the Old Trafford were approved by the Stretford District Council on 2 March 1909, although there were one or two conditions attached to this, such as the widening of Warwick Road and the railway bridge to be carried out at the same time. So it was Manchester United Football

Club Old Trafford on top of the letterheads from now on, and it was all systems go to have the new stadium ready for the visit of Lancashire neighbours Liverpool, on Saturday 19 February 1910, for the inaugural match. This should really have been the second fixture at the new ground, with the visit of Tottenham Hotspur on 22 January scheduled for the opening match. However, with work on various sections of the stadium still incomplete, the supporters had to wait just a little longer to meander through the cobbled streets to their new home ground.

Traffic was particularly heavy in the Stretford area on the day of the Liverpool match, as all imaginable forms of transport headed towards Old Trafford, with those not fortunate enough to own, be able to pay for or be offered a lift on a vehicle of some sort, making their way on foot.

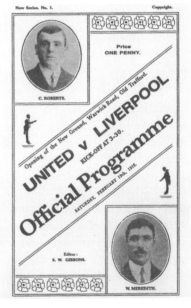

Above: An Old Trafford aerial shot.

Right: The United *v.* Liverpool official programme, including portraits of Charlie Roberts and William Meredith.

Below: A game at Old Trafford in the 1930s.

Admission was 6d (just over 2p) for the ground and 1s (5p), 1s 6d (just over 7p) and 2s (10p) for the covered stand. There were also a few reserved seats in the centre of the stand for those who could afford the 5s (25p). Those who could afford the luxury of a seat in the stand were pleasantly impressed upon their arrival, as the seats were no wooden benches, but plush tip-up affairs to which they were shown by attendants. It was, as one supporter commented, 'more like the theatre than football'.

As kick-off time approached, it was not easy to estimate the actual attendance inside, but outside, both around the ground and on the approach roads, it was quite obvious that both the gatemen at the turnstiles and the Manchester Tramways were having difficulty in coping with the vast crowds. Today, the record books give an attendance at a rounded up 45,000, but it is to be believed that around 5,000 more managed to gain illegal entry by various means, including a small, unfinished window fanlight.

So, the lush green turf with its vivid white line markings looked immaculate as the sun shone down on it, with the red-and-white quartered corner flags fluttering in the afternoon breeze. The surroundings were all something of a dream for however many were indeed present – but they were soon brought back down to reality with a bump, as the visitors won 4-3, fighting back from 2-0 down.

Within fifteen minutes of the kick-off, Sandy Turnbull had the ball in the back of the net following a Dick Duckworth free-kick, as had Homer, following through on a Harold Halse shot which the Liverpool goalkeeper failed to hold, to give United a two-goal advantage.

The visitors began to regain some of the play and soon pulled a goal back, but the two-goal advantage was soon re-established when George Wall scored with a fine shot from an oblique angle out on the left. Despite this further setback, the white-shirted Liverpool players refused to give in and their resilience was rewarded as they began to get the better of the United defence.

Goddard soon made it 3-2. Stewart equalised and then scored what was to be the winner near the end, as the rain began to fall on the subdued spectators, making it not the best of starts. But with the surroundings just as unfamiliar to the United players as they were to the visitors, it was not what could have been otherwise considered a shock defeat.

Having got the initial fixture out of the way, things could now only become easier in the day-to-day running of the club. There was still a considerable amount of work to be done, but it was not long before the new stadium was being acknowledged as one of the best, if not the best in the country.

The construction of Old Trafford had created something of a burden on the club's finances, with those at the helm having to juggle the pounds and pence off the pitch. Matters on the pitch did not exactly keep the turnstiles clicking merrily away, with the club dropping from the First Division to the Second, at the end of season 1921/22.

By 1926/27 the financial situation had somewhat improved, with the overdraft at the bank having been reduced from £3,355 to zero. Attendances had increased with the return of First Division football in 1925, a local 'derby' match with Manchester City attracting 48,657, while a fifth-round FA Cup replay against Sunderland was watched by 58,661, paying £4,823. Everything looked rosy and the board of directors decided, after much debate, to purchase the freehold of Old Trafford, held under the Manchester Brewery Company, which at the time was costing £1,300 per year in rent and rates. The proposed sale was agreed and on 25 March 1927, it was completed, although the business was overshadowed by the death of Mr J. H. Davies, the club's benefactor. His presence and expertise was greatly missed in the boardroom, and once again, the club began to struggle.

As the 1930s dawned they proved to be something of a trying time for the club, and at one point the directors had to approach the Brewery to ask if they could defer their mortgage interest payments, while at the same time asking the Stretford Urban District Council for permission to pay road charges by instalments. With problems at the bank mounting to a serious level, a solution to the problem had to be found, and towards the end of 1931 a local clothing entrepreneur, Mr J. W. Gibson, met the board, set out a plan for recovery and invested some £30,000 into the club.

The problems, however, were far from over, as off the field they were fortunate to avoid relegation to the Third Division at the end of season 1933/34, which would have been the ultimate embarrassment. There were further problems on the horizon, as by the summer of 1940 Britain became more involved in the war in Europe due to the capitulation of France in July of that year. But despite this, the Football League once again decided to continue their War League fixtures for the forthcoming season, a decision that was to cause United numerous problems that would take almost a decade to overcome.

Christmas Day 1940 should have seen Stockport County visit Old Trafford for a North Regional League match, but on the night of Sunday 22 December German aircraft bombed Trafford Park, with the Old Trafford ground sustaining damage, as did the industrial area surrounding it. During those air raids over 300 Mancunians were killed.

The Stockport match was hastily switched to County's ground and the following scheduled Old Trafford fixture, against Blackburn Rovers on 28 December, was also switched to Stockport. Playing those two home fixtures at Stockport did not have too much of an effect on attendances, with 1,500 watching the Blackburn fixture (a 5-5 draw), and home attendances having ranged between 700 and 3,000, although the 'derby' fixture brought 10,000.

Old Trafford was tidied up and home fixtures at their rightful venue were resumed in both the Lancashire Cup and the League War Cup. The North Regional League fixtures resumed on 8 March with a match against Bury, when hat-tricks from Rowley and Carey, along with a single Smith goal, brought a 7-3 victory, thrilling a 3,000 crowd. This, however, was to be the last competitive match to be played at Old Trafford until 1949, as the night of 11 March saw yet another sustained German air attack on Manchester, causing yet more damage and devastation, with Trafford Park once again the prime target of the bombers. Once again, the stadium suffered severe damage, losing most of the Main Stand, dressing rooms and offices. This time there could be no patch-up job, and the club moved to temporary office accommodation a short distance from the ground at Cornbrook Cold Stores, which were owned by Mr J. W. Gibson, where club affairs were continued by secretary Walter Crickmer.

Manchester United Football Club were now homeless, and while arrangements were being made with the Stretford Corporation to dismantle what was left of the stand and salvage the steel, along with demolishing other unsafe parts of the ground, claims for war damage to property were put forward to the authorities. This was all very well in the long term, but what was to happen in the meantime, with half a season fixtures still to fulfil?

Assistance came from neighbours City, who offered their unfortunate rivals a helping hand suggesting that they used their Maine Road ground for 'home' fixtures until the time came when Old Trafford was playable again. It was a lifeline United needed and grasped thankfully, as they were determined to continue with their fixtures as best they could. Following clearance from the Football League, Maine Road became 'home' for both the Blue and the Red factions of Manchester.

In August 1945, the War Damage Commission granted the club a sum of £4,800 to clear the debris around the ground, with a further £17,478 being granted later towards the rebuilding of the stand. Those payments were made in instalments, with the final sum of just over £710 for the demolition work not being paid until February 1954. Local youngsters earned themselves some extra pocket money by painstakingly walking up and down the pitch picking up broken glass.

Despite being uncertain as to what funds were being made available to them, the difficult job of pulling down the entire Main Stand (or what was left of it), along with the wall behind it, was carried out in April 1945. During the summer of that year, the wall was rebuilt and new dressing rooms were erected. Repair work on the covered section on the opposite side of the ground was also carried out, with the playing surface, although in reasonable and playable condition, was given 300 tons of special soil with new turf being laid down its centre from one goalmouth to the other.

United had hoped to kick-off season 1946/47, under the guidance of manager Matt Busby who had taken over the reins on 19 February 1945, back in familiar surroundings instead of the shared accommodation at Maine Road. However, the club accounts for season 1945/46 mentions that 'owing to the persistent acute shortage of building materials it had not been possible to reinstate the club premises and they would continue to use Manchester City's ground'. Some 30,000 did squeeze into the ground in early August to watch a Reds *v.* Blues practice match, which ended in a 3-3 draw, while both United and City reserve teams played their Central League fixtures there. The more serious business of League football was, however, still played a few miles away.

In the opening United match programme for season 1946/47 against Grimsby Town, Chairman Mr J. W. Gibson wrote:

> A lump rises in my throat when I think of our premises at Old Trafford damaged beyond repair by fire and blast in March 1941 and still looking a sorry spectacle owing to government policy of issuing only limited licences for building materials while the housing problem is so manifest.

By December, plans had been drawn up for the proposed 'new look' Old Trafford once permission was given. The architect's drawing gave the impression of large covered stands and spacious terracing, accompanied by up-to-date facilities for the players. It was hoped the capacity could rise to around 125,000 with the railway station, now fully operational alongside the ground providing quick and easy access to and from it. But could the ideas on paper be transferred onto brick and concrete?

The Main Stand, damaged by German bombs in the 1940s.

With Manchester City enjoying the extra income from the attendances that United attracted at Maine Road, the reserve-team fixtures at Old Trafford never produced 'ground full' notices or anywhere near it. However, on 6 June 1947, the Old Trafford gates were firmly locked with 36,000 inside, having purchased their tickets weeks before, allowing them to watch Salford Schoolboys play Leicester Schoolboys in the English Schools FA final replay. The Salford schools had been more than happy with their 0-0 draw against the current holders in the first match, but a venue for the replay looked as though it might cause them a problem. Earlier-round ties had been played at United's The Cliff training ground, but such was the interest in the final, a larger venue was required and following consultation with the local constabulary, a 36,000 all-ticket limit was put on Old Trafford and a strong police presence was prominent at the ground to prevent spectators encroaching on the bomb-damaged areas.

November 1948 saw City give United give notice to quit Maine Road, as they were beginning to find it somewhat restricted with both clubs continuing to share the ground. Whether or not United had suggested the idea to their neighbours in order to help push forward their plans for the further reconstruction of Old Trafford, as they were becoming a little exasperated with the limited progress, is not recorded. The slow progress in refurbishing the ground also annoyed the United support, with one, a Mr H. S. Thompson of Stockport, going as far as to organise a petition, in the hope of persuading the Ministry of Works to expedite the issue of licences for the restoration of Old Trafford. Mr Thompson had already approached Members of Parliament and had between 200 and 300 fellow supporters standing by ready to help with any work involved at the ground.

By the end of 1949, the final remnants of war damage had been removed and the levelling and concreting of the stand area begun. A section was made into concrete terracing and some wooden cinema-type seats were procured to accommodate around 3,000, all without cover. Who would care? Being back home would be enough for club and supporters alike. Some cover was provided, but this was only for a select few, such as the directors and the press, with a corrugated-iron awning constructed over their respective boxes in an attempt to keep out any inclement weather.

So, at 6.30 p.m. on Wednesday 24 August 1949, United ran out onto the Old Trafford lush green turf, to face local Lancashire rivals Bolton Wanderers, for what was the first League fixture at the ground since 1939. In the club programme for the match, chairman Mr J. W. Gibson wrote that he was grieved that he could not welcome back supporters to the fully developed stadium which he had in mind, but he hoped to do something about the stand before the following season.

As the 1950s began to unfold, attendances had begun to rise and Old Trafford was slowly becoming the place to be on a Saturday afternoon. But what did the United supporter of the mid-fifties have to pay to watch his favourites? Admission to the ground was 2s (10p), juniors 9d (4p). The covered terrace 3s 6d (18p), juniors' 2s (10p). Unreserved seats in A and E blocks were 5s (25p), while reserved seats in B and C were 6s 5d (33p). A season ticket for Stand 'B' would have put you back the grand sum of £6 10s (£6.50p). For those parting with their hard-earned cash at the turnstiles on the opening day of season 1955/56, grandstand patrons had the added bonus of some 3,000 extra seats after some reconstruction work which also provided new refreshment bars below sections A and E. Around the ground, other work had been carried out during the summer break, which led to up to date offices, reconditioned dressing rooms and recreational facilities for the players.

Manager Matt Busby had set his sights on not simply competing against England's top clubs but also those from Europe and had, against the wishes of the Football League, entered the 1956/57 European Cup competition. However, they once again had to turn to neighbour's City

Above left: The *United Review*, 1949/50.

Above right: Manchester United *v.* Bolton Wanderers, 1957.

for the use of their Maine Road ground for the opening rounds, as Old Trafford, unlike many other grounds, did not have floodlights.

This was soon on the agenda and they were used for the first time when Lancashire neighbours Bolton Wanderers visited on 23 March 1957. This gave Bolton the distinction of being the first visitors after the war and also the first to play under the new lights. The night sky around Old Trafford was bright in the evening air, with the illuminated glow from the new lights (three of which were situated outside the stadium walls), as the supporters made their way towards the ground, attracted like moths, as they hurried on their way.

During season 1958/59 more junior turnstiles were opened at the Stretford End in order to admit the growing number of youngsters wanting to attend games with a little more ease. That particular end of the ground came in for more alterations during the summer of 1959, when work began on a new covered stand which would hold over 12,000 supporters. This improvement would also provide cover for the 22,000 who stood in this section admission to this new stand would be 2s (10p). It was also during this season that all seating at the ground was made bookable in advance for first-team fixtures.

Numerous suggestions had been put forward for a lasting memorial to those who had lost their lives at Munich to be erected at the ground. Some had gone as far as to suggest that sections of the ground should be called after individual players, but this particular idea was turned down by the board. In the end, a large memorial plaque was decided upon, which was to be sited outside the main entrance on the railway side of the ground, while the ground committee were to have a special clock made for a site at the Warwick Road end. A small plaque bearing the names of the journalists who died was to be installed in the Press Box by the Football Writers Association.

On 25 February 1960, the rain poured down from a dark Manchester sky, as some 1,250 invited guests, including United players and directors, along with parents, relatives and friends of those who had died in the disaster, stood silently as manager Matt Busby pulled back the purple drapes which hung over the Munich memorial plaque. Clearly moved by the occasion, the United manager said, 'I know that those who are near and dear have a memorial in their hearts which will last for all time. But now our many friends will also have an everlasting memorial here to the lads who helped make this such a great club.'

The plaque, designed by a local architect M. L. Vipond, and constructed by Messrs Jaconello Ltd of Manchester, showed a complete plan of the ground measuring 7 feer 9 inches by 6 feet. Green slabs of faience marked out the pitch incised with black-and-gold glass letters forming an inscription and names of those who lost their lives. The terraces, gangways and steps were also in faience to scale, and were in a memorial colour of mauve and grey. The stand roofs and perimeter path had been worked from solid quartzite, enclosed by red Balmoral granite forming the boundary wall of the ground. Two teak figures representing a player and spectator stood either side of a laurel wreath and ball, inscribed 1958.

The second of the memorials, a clock, which was sited at the Warwick Road end, facing the main road leading to the ground. Above and below the two-faced dial was the inscription – 6 February 1958, Munich. This was unveiled by Mr Dan Marsden the chairman of the ground committee, while the bronze plaque in the press box, bearing the names of the eight journalists who died was unveiled by the only surviving journalist, Mr Frank Taylor.

The club were now beginning to find that the costs of ground improvements and refurbishments were becoming increasingly hard to bear as, despite the recent success, money was not exactly flowing into the club's bank account. Discussions took place at boardroom level regarding ways and means of reducing such costs, while at the same time keep the ground up to date and in pristine condition. It was those discussions that prompted a visit, in March 1961, to Edgbaston cricket ground in Birmingham, the home of Warwickshire CCC, who had set up a successful football pools competition, which successfully made a profit of over £70,000 per year. Following the visit, further discussions took place at Old Trafford and it was decided to set up something similar, entitled the Manchester United Development Association, an organisation which, while offering the supporters an opportunity to win sums of money through a football pools style operation, would also help finance further ground improvements. As time would tell, it would prove to have been an invaluable innovation.

Not only did United take the idea of the pools competition from Warwickshire, they also prised away the assistant organiser of their pools, Bill Burke. Under the guidance of the aforementioned

The stadium in the 1960s.

gentleman, and from his small office inside Old Trafford, he began bringing in much needed revenue, starting in August 1961, with prize money of £240. It was not long before the enterprise bore fruit, with the Development Association's first contribution to ground improvement being the installation of 700 wooden seats at the back of the Stretford End terrace, which became Stand E. These seats were used for the first time on 25 September 1962, when Portuguese club Benfica, the current European Cup holders, visited Manchester for a friendly fixture.

The year 1963 brought the announcement that England were to host the 1966 World Cup and the United directors were honoured by the selection of Old Trafford as one of the stadiums that would be a venue for some of the fixtures in Group C. This prompted the board to put their plans for further ground development into motion, and it was announced in December that the club were to build a £250,000 cantilever stand along the United Road side of the ground. 'New Trafford – as it will be after the £250,000 investment in soccer's future', proclaimed the *Daily Mail*, with a *Sportsmail*'s artist's impression of the new stand superimposed onto an aerial view of the present ground.

Although prompting enthusiastic comments from the United support, the illustration of the architect's drawing that had appeared in the *Manchester Evening News and Chronicle* the previous day, made the new construction look even more imposing. Alongside this, the paper's United correspondent David Meek wrote:

> Manchester United are to have an elegant, £25,000 cantilever stand at Old Trafford. Work will start at the end of the season on what will be the longest and most advanced stand in the country. It will go up opposite the Main Stand in place of the old covering over the terracing. There will be 10,500 seats and covered standing room for 10,000 more. The cantilever roof will project to the front of the terracing where it will be 48ft high. It will be suspended from steel tubes retained from concrete yokes projecting 30ft above the rear of the stand. All seats will have a clear, uninterrupted view of the game.
>
> The architects, Mather and Nutter, of Manchester, have prepared a preliminary scheme and are starting ground investigation immediately. Building will start next summer and be completed in fifteen months, they hope, for the start of the 1965/66 season. This will give United use of the stand in good time for the World Cup in 1966. It is, in fact, the plan for this new stand that clinched Old Trafford as a choice of venue for the World Cup in favour of Maine Road.
>
> The stand, which will be 660ft long, will run the whole length of the ground and will turn at the corners. At the Streford end it will link up with the existing stand extension, though there will be a slight gap for the floodlighting pylon. At the Stretford end, the corner will also be included in the stand. The new development will not mean a reduction in the capacity of Old Trafford. New techniques will be used to take the stand further back so that spectators will be sitting over the entrances.

The building of this new stand was a matter of careful consideration, as it left no funds for strengthening the playing squad, which obviously took priority over any structural matters. Manager Matt Busby, however, felt that his squad was strong enough to challenge for the games honours and gave the okay for the money to be spent on the stand, instead of being left in the bank in case he wanted to make any new signings.

Perhaps the most prominent feature of this new construction, but one that was not mentioned in David Meek's article, would be the installation of thirty-four private boxes, which could each hold up to six people. The reason for there being no mention in David's article was that they

United Road in the 1980s.

were not a feature of the original plans. It was only after Bill Burke managed to persuade United directors to visit Manchester racecourse to see a previous Mather & Nutter construction, one containing private boxes, and then view the pitch from the back of the semi-constructed stand at Old Trafford, that the board decided to go along with the idea. Whether the added bonus of each director being given three boxes swung the matter is not recorded.

These top-of-the-range facilities would be taken by businesses to entertain clients. A waiter service would be available, with a private lift to transfer those fortunate to have the use of them from ground level to the heated boxes via a lounge. Centre boxes were to be let at £300 for a season, with those at the side £250. The rental secured admission to all home games and needless to say, all boxes were over-applied for from the start.

An early estimated cost for constructing the new stand was £175,000, but a closer examination took the figure up to £250,000. The final cost, however, was nearer to £320,000, and with only around £75,000 in the bank at this time it was a major undertaking, putting the club well into the red, although the Development Association eventually paid most of the costs. Throughout the summer, work continued around Old Trafford, with the World Cup now less than a year away and becoming much more of a priority to United. By the time season 1965/66 arrived, a large section of the new cantilever stand was ready for occupation, with the final section at the Warwick Road end scheduled to be available in October. Work also had to be carried out below the stand, with alterations to the toilet and refreshment areas adding to the expenditure. Better facilities for the supporters, but what sort of prices did the United fan of the mid-sixties have to pay to sit in what would be known as Stands G and H, or stand in the United Road Paddock, in front of this new construction? To sit in sections G and H, it would cost 10s (50p) and 12s 6d (63p), bookable two weeks in advance, while the Paddock was 5s (25p), with no reductions for juniors!

Throughout the sixties and into the seventies, crowd trouble had reared its ugly head, with United's large following having more than its fair share of troublemakers. Old Trafford was once again under construction as the seventies dawned, with the cantilever stand on the United Road being extended round behind the Scoreboard End of the ground at a cost of £400,000. A knife-throwing incident against Newcastle United on 27 February 1971 led to an area of the Stretford End being closed off, and the club was fined £7,000 and being forced to play their first two home

Redeveloping the Scoreboard
End in the 1970s.

games of season 1971/72 on neutral venues. Anfield, Liverpool and the Victoria Ground, Stoke, were eventually chosen.

On the playing front, United had struggled during the new decade, with Wilf McGuinness and Frank O'Farrell both being sacked before Tommy Docherty became manager. Under the high-profile Scot, things changed little, and having just managed to avoid the drop down into the Second Division at the end of season 1972/73, they were once again involved in a struggle against relegation twelve months later.

With the minutes ticking away and victory essential in order to maintain their top-flight status, former United favourite Denis Law, now a City player after having been given a free transfer by Docherty, back-heeled the ball past a stranded Alex Stepney in the United goal. Almost immediately, large numbers of supporters surged onto the pitch, but were eventually forced back behind the barriers, allowing the game to restart.

Soon afterwards, a second pitch invasion occurred and, despite an announcement by Matt Busby and with four minutes of the game remaining, the referee took the players off the pitch and, following the advice of the police inspector in charge, abandoned the game. This led to even more spectators coming onto the pitch and they began to assemble in front of the Main Stand at the mouth of the tunnel, where a line of twenty policemen prevented anyone from going any further.

Over 200 had been ejected from the ground before and during the match on a shameful day in the club's history, and it was they – along with those who had on several occasions invaded the pitch – who made the newspaper headlines in the days that followed. Calls were made to close the ground and a record punishment looked to be coming United's way as the afternoon's events began to be digested. Sir Matt Busby said that perhaps cages of some kind would be a solution. The final match of the season, at Stoke a few days later, saw further trouble from United supporters and club officials began a nervous close season waiting to see what punishment would be handed out.

The Football League later confirmed that the 1-0 scoreline would stand, and in June the United directors decided to take matters into their own hands rather than await the FA's decision, and announced that they would be erecting 9-foot-high spiked fences behind each goal at a cost of £4,500. A five-man FA disciplinary commission visited Old Trafford and were shown two

The Stretford End.

specimen sections of the fencing, with safety gates added in case of an emergency. The commission were satisfied with United's move and simply ordered the club to pay their costs, which amounted to less than £200.

So, those attending the opening fixture of 1974/75 at Old Trafford were greeted with the unfamiliar sight of the metal fencing behind either goal. It was perhaps a deterrent of sorts at Old Trafford, but trouble, however, continued at away games, something that United could do little to prevent.

Before the end of 1974, work began on redeveloping the Main Stand, which would incorporate an executive suite and two restaurants, with a total outlay of around £500,000, plus a further £70,000 on décor. By the beginning of the following season 1975/76, the Executive Suite Restaurant and Grill Room were catering for members of the public as well as supplying a superb *á la carte* menu on match days in the former, while the latter catered for those with more simple tastes. The same facilities were also available at lunch times during the week as well as non-match weekends, while they could also be hired for banquets, conferences and any other private function. This provided the club with extra revenue, with the Executive Suite having a limited membership of 300, at a cost of £135, soon being oversubscribed.

In 1977, the Executive Suite was extended with the opening of the Jubilee Room next to the Grill Room. This area saw the beginning of match sponsorship packages, with the sponsors and up to fifty guests receiving a champagne buffet prior to a match. On weekdays, the room was used for meetings, small exhibitions and private lunches.

The building of the Executive Suite, a further £70,000 on to the bill, had involved extending out from behind the Main Stand, still enabling team coaches etc. to drive down that side of the ground. It did, however, destroy a familiar landmark – the Munich Memorial Plaque, which had been situated above the main entrance. Upon the completion of the new extension, only part of the plaque was still visible. It had been originally planned to remove the plaque and relocate it, but when attempts were made to do so it was discovered to be to firmly attached to the outer wall and could not be removed in one piece. So, with only one alternative, the club commissioned a new memorial, identical to the original, which would be sited on the brick wall of K stand at the Scoreboard End of the ground in full view of anyone approaching the ground.

The 1957 FA Cup final playing kit of Duncan Edwards in the old Museum.

Despite the somewhat lack of success in the seventies and eighties, the club's following, however despised it was in many quarters, was the envy of many, and the directors were continuously looking at ways and means to extend the ground's capacity. November 1984 saw plans put before the Trafford Borough Council's Planning Committee to redevelop the old Scoreboard Paddock section of the ground. This project, which would create stand L, would provide a further 1,800 seats and fifteen executive boxes inside the stadium, with a new ticket office on the outside. It was also hoped to incorporate a form of club museum in this section. In the club programme, the *United Review*, for 22 February 1986, supporters were given their first look at those plans and in the following five issues of the programme, an artist's impression of how the concept might look was included. Since the idea was first mentioned, numerous items had been handed in to swell the already large collection of trophies and memorabilia assembled by the club over the years. Obviously there would not be enough room to display everything, but the showcases in the museum would cover the complete history of the club from the days as Newton Heath to the present, and would include everything from shirts and contracts, to medals and match tickets. Interactive displays featuring videos and computers were early suggestions for sections of the museum, but the sheer volume of items made this impractical if as much as possible was going to be displayed. Those supporters who could not get enough of the club eagerly awaited the Aladdin's cave of United memorabilia.

The doors of the museum, situated above the Sir Matt Busby Suite, eventually opened on Thursday 1 May 1986, when club president Sir Matt Busby, along with local civic dignitaries, present and former players, plus other special guests, including Duncan Edwards' mother, watched club chairman Martin Edwards cut the ribbon on the £100,000 development, a concept originally suggested by the late director Denzil Haroun.

Although money once again seemed to be no problem for the club, they always welcomed the lump sums available in the forms of grants for ground improvements. In early February, the Football Trust awarded the club £132,000 to help pay for the installation of seats in the North Stand Lower. It was hoped the sum of around £2 million would follow at a later date when the Stretford End would be turned into an all-seated section, at a cost of around £13 million. An additional £1 million was also paid out in the summer of 1991 to install seating in front of stands B and C and replacing existing seating in F, G, H and I. The latter would be done in red and white making the word 'Manchester', with the 'United' on the seats in the lower section.

The Stretford End.

Two areas within the stadium and situated below the Main Stand were scheduled to move with the completion of the new Stretford End stand – the player's lounge and the dressing rooms. The former could be considered rather plain and little different from a lounge bar in a hotel, although one distinctive feature was a large honours board containing the names of all the players who had represented the club at international level in the post-war years. On the other hand, the dressing rooms, although not identical, would be of an impressively high standard and would be able to accommodate twenty-two players and managerial team comfortably.

On the evening of Thursday 20 January 1994, the football world was stunned by the announcement that Sir Matt Busby had died. The man, who more than any other was responsible for the worldwide adoration of the club and the magnificent stadium it called home, would no more be seen on a match day, walking slowly across the forecourt, with members of his family, to the acknowledgement of the supporters, as he went to watch his beloved team. For many, Sir Matt *was* Manchester United, and vice versa, and as the news broke across the city, supporters began to arrive at the ground, simply to pay their respects to the great man. Some laid bunches of flowers against the wall of the stadium, underneath the Munich memorial, while others left their scarves. The following day saw countless others make the same pilgrimage and the forecourt was soon a carpet of flowers, scarves and memorabilia. Inside the museum was a book of remembrance for the fans to sign, and there was also a small area given over to a large photograph of Sir Matt along with numerous flowers and wreaths.

Saturday 22 January was match day at Old Trafford and it had been obvious over the last couple of days that it would be no ordinary one. From early morning, there are always people scattered around the ground, but today there were more than usual. Television crews mingled with the increasing numbers on the forecourt as the carpet of scarves, flowers, photographs and the like, took on new dimensions. As 3 p.m. approached, those with match tickets were already inside, determined for once not to be late, while outside there were still around an estimated 15,000, content at simply just being there on the day. Manchester United paid its last respects to its president.

As an announcement from the public address system asked the crowd to stand, the first strains of bagpipes could be heard from the mouth of the players tunnel down in the corner of the

A colour aerial shot of the stadium with the North Stand still under construction.

Stretford End. The haunting melody of 'A Scottish Soldier' grew louder as the lone piper led the players of United and Everton onto the pitch, followed by officials of both clubs. There were lumps in many throats and numerous tears were unashamedly shed. With the piper now silent, and both teams lined up in the centre of the pitch, an eerie silence fell on the ground. Following the respected silence, the United supporters in the 44,750 crowd applauded the Everton followers for their show of respect.

By mid-November 1995, the plans for the new towering second tier to be added onto the North Stand were on show at Trafford Borough Council. The construction, which would dwarf the rest of the stadium, would reach almost 160 feet in height, making it around 94 feet higher than the existing stand. In order to build such a structure, United Road would have to be altered, as it would extend some 60 feet outwards. A new access road would need to be built, and a further ninety full- and part-time jobs would be created to service the new construction. Club secretary, Ken Ramsden confirmed that United were in negotiations with Trafford Park Estates to purchase the land required to implement the plans. Two months later, the Trafford Park Development Corporation had approved the plans and the Trafford Council were in agreement towards the triple-decker development.

The plans, once again, had not been straightforward for the club, as some angry clashes had occurred between rival factions on the council, who felt that local residents were perhaps not being considered as the club was increasing its capacity and bringing more people into the area on match days. The imagination of locally based supporters could at last ease back to normality, as on Tuesday 17 March the front page of the *Manchester Evening News* carried a photograph of the scale model of the new super stadium, following chairman Martin Edwards' announcement that, 'the biggest, most costly and the most ambitious development ever undertaken by Manchester United', would go ahead eight days after planning permission had been given.

With the club given the green light, the project team was put together, consisting of construction manager Hilston Laurie, architect Atherden Fuller, structural engineer Campbell Reith Hill, mechanical engineer W. E. Hannan, and electrical engineer Piggot and Whitfield. The team had been together for the Stretford End development, with the architects having been responsible for the original cantilever stand on United Road in 1965.

An empty United Road, with cranes in the background.

Tim Laycock, regional director of Hilston Laurie, revealed that the team's original proposals were to construct a new two-tier stand, cantilevered over the top of the existing North Stand, simply to increase the ground capacity, but they were concerned that the thirty year old construction would prove too expensive to redesign to modem standards. With United very much concerned on providing first class amenities for their supporters and improving safety, the team decided to put forward a proposal to demolish the whole stand and replace it with a new steel construction. Even that was not completely straightforward, as thirteen different proposals were considered before the final decision was made.

For those interested in the minutest detail, the stand would measure 114 metres long by 60 metres wide, rising 45 metres above the pitch at its highest point. The roof would be constructed in tubular sections, made up into sixteen main roof trusses measuring 66 metres long and tapering in depth from 9.8 metres to 2 metres. Some 3,500 tonnes of steel would be used, along with 4,500 tonnes of concrete in the form of 10,000 square meters of pre-cast seating units which would take one 185 wagons to deliver. A total of 14,800 individual pieces of steel were to be incorporated!

The three tiers would be divided into eight seating levels, with 10,000 square meters earmarked for restaurants and a new museum. Fans in the top tier would sit at a steep 34 degree angle above the horizontal, while the second tier would be a mere 30 degrees. The cost of the development was expected to be around £28 million, with some £9.1 million of that total going towards the purchase of land along the United Road that would be straddled by the new stand. This was actually almost £3 million more than the market value. Seating 25,111, the Old Trafford capacity would rise to 55,300, thus becoming the largest club stadium in the country. This would include thirty-two private boxes, with increased seating in the lower sections. The only negative points about the plans was that the next season would see a reduced ground capacity to a mere 33,000, with almost all of those being season ticket and League match ticket holders, leaving little or no space for the ordinary club member.

As well as increasing the seating capacity, a look at the early plans for the new construction showed that it would also incorporate numerous other facilities. On level one, there would be a bar dining area, along with part of the new club museum, although the main part of the museum

Old Trafford.

would be on level two and would incorporate a classroom and a cinema. There will also be another dining area with kitchen. Level three would also house part of the museum, an executive suite, box-holders' lounge and bar, another kitchen and the Red Café, a theme restaurant. The final fourth level would also provide further dining facilities.

The Hilston Laurie contract would be dictated by five stages, and as each stage was completed it was hoped to be able to release further seating to the supporters, with the entire job scheduled for completion in April 1996.

Prior to the United *v.* Chelsea fixture on 2 November 1996, a plaque was unveiled in the players tunnel area in memory of Mr James Gibson, who had come to the club's rescue in December 1931, ploughing £3,000 into the funds. The figure, a modest amount by today's standards, was enough to keep the club afloat, providing some secure footing on which to build; with the club quite possibly not being in need of a stadium like today's if it had not been for his investment. A member of the Gibson family had maintained a place on the United board from 1931 until 1996 and the death of James Gibson's son Alan. Another plaque in Gibson's honour can be found on the railway bridge leading onto or from what is now Sir Matt Busby Way.

A similar plaque was unveiled opposite this a couple of months later, this time in memory of Mr John Henry Davies, who had rescued the club from bankruptcy during season 1901/02, while also playing a major part in the change of name from Newton Heath to Manchester United.

The James Gibson plaque on
Railway Bridge.

The statue of Sir Matt Busby.

On Friday 26 April 1996, a giant crane moved onto the Old Trafford forecourt, to manoeuvre an 11-foot-high bronze statue of Sir Matt Busby onto a podium below the Munich Memorial, on the roof of the entrance into the executive boxes facing Sir Matt Busby Way. The specially commissioned statue, weighing more than a ton, was the work of sculptor Philip Jackson. Inside the hollow figure were some of the scarves, shirts, etc., which had been placed on the forecourt following the great man's death. The following day, a special ceremony was held when members of Sir Matt's family, civic dignitaries and club officials were present at the unveiling.

The new-look museum, which had cost £4 million and taken around seven months to complete, was built on three floors and would be the new starting point for the stadium tours was officially opened on 11 April 1998. Incorporating its own café, shop and audio visual theatre, the museum contained a mixture of traditional showcase displays, along with graphic, historical and contemporary film footage, as well as modern techniques to involve visitors of all ages.

The displays would also incorporate much of the material collected by the club and previously hidden away in storage and would be incorporated into a number of themes, including 'The Trophy Room', 'Legends', 'Munich', 'Playing Kits' and the likes. There would also be an archive for researchers and a dedicated classroom to reflect the demand of schools and groups.

But still Old Trafford continued to grow, with plans to redevelop the East and West Stands (the Scoreboard End and the Stretford End to the die-hards), were soon before the Trafford Council

Planning Committee, a move that would increase the capacity to 67,000. United certainly had no fears in reaching their objective with regards to filling Old Trafford for every home fixture. The new seating in the East Stand was used for the first time in January 2000, while the new upper section of the West Stand was completed during the summer of 2000. For the opening fixture of season 2000/01, against Newcastle United, the attendance was recorded at 67,477 and it only dropped below the 67,000 mark for the Champions League fixtures. The highest attendance was recorded against Coventry City on 14 April, with 67,637 present for the 4-2 victory, a win which left the players and spectators waiting three hours to find out if they were to be champions again.

The chase for the championship obviously created a wealth of exciting moments, while at the same time causing considerable problems as a majority of supporters continued to stand during matches and not simply when their red heroes were on the attack. As in the previous campaign, United marched through both group phases in the Champions League into the quarter-finals, where Bayern Munich were waiting with thoughts of revenge. But as United sought to gain advantage in the first-leg home fixture, the horizon was darkened with thoughts of a much different kind, as Trafford Council threatened to close part of the ground if the team reached the semi-final stage. Town Hall chiefs insisted that supporters left them with no choice after continuously breaking safety regulations by standing and if the semi-finals were indeed reached, then the upper section of the West Stand would be closed. At the time of the announcement, it had not been decided if the whole of the stand, or only a certain number of seats would be affected, but the *Manchester Evening News* believed that it would only be around 1,000 seats at the front of that particular stand.

As it was, the council did not have to worry about a supporter's backlash, as the decision was taken away from them when Bayern Munich followed up their 1-0 victory in Manchester with a 2-1 win back in Germany, knocking United out of the competition.

Old Trafford began to rival town and city centres due to the number of statues and memorial plaques sited around the ground, with the latest addition being unveiled prior to the home match with Aston Villa. Situated with the West Stand, Denis Law paid something of a rare visit to the ground to unveil a 10-foot-tall statue of himself, sculpted by Ben Panting and situated on the concourse of the upper tier of the stand. Plans were also revealed in March 2004 regarding the filling in of the north-east and north-west quadrants, which would see the ground capacity increased to approximately 75,000 and in early February 2005, the Trafford Metropolitan Borough Council agreed to United's proposed plans. To gain such permission, United had to satisfy the council of certain aspects of the new developments, as local residents, as they had been in the past, were not altogether too happy to have a further 7,500 people on their doorsteps every other week.

One local councillor, Beverley Hughes, criticised the club, saying, 'I think local people are just exasperated, because they want to meet the club half way, but they've got a history of broken promises and because of that, local people are just very cynical about this.' Another councillor felt that the increased number of cars in the area would cause a problem, as would the amount of litter. United's group property manager, George Johnstone, revealed that 'it was a long process, involving detailed negotiations with the local authority'.

We agreed on a package of measures to reduce the impact on the transport system and the local community. We have made a commitment to contribute £1 million over a ten-year period, with the first payment to be made when the new seating is fully licensed.

Having secured the permission, it was now all systems go, with contractors sending in tenders for the work. As George explained:

> Until we have appointed a main contractor, we can't be clear about specific details. But it is our intention that building work will not affect the current stadium capacity although we can't rule out losing some seats at certain stages of the project. The scoreboards will have to be relocated, but our aim will be to ensure that everybody inside the ground can still see a scoreboard.
>
> We are grateful to supporters for their patience and understanding during the preparatory work, and we'll be asking fans to please bear with us during the construction work. Once the redevelopment is complete and the gables have been removed, the new configuration will make for an improved atmosphere. The new bowl effect will allow noise to roll around the stadium rather than being trapped in specific stands as at present.

The redevelopment was of course about much more than adding a few more red seats to the stadium interior. The outside of the ground would also take on a 'new look', with towers at either end, which would be the structural element of the quadrants, designed in such a way that they would give it a modern appearence. It would also make Old Trafford the third-largest stadium in Britain, behind the new Wembley (90,000) and Twickenham (which was due to increase to 80,000).

On the evening of Friday 25 November 2005, Old Trafford was a hive of activity, as countless supporters were once again found assembling outside the ground, opposite the Megastore and Sir Matt Busby statue. On this occasion, however, United were not playing. Indeed, there was no game. There was silence, the cold night air carrying no cries of discontent against the American owners or terrace anthems; only a muffled sob could be heard from time to time. A small bunch of flowers, a scarf, a photograph were placed along the wall in front of the car park, soon to be joined by countless others, as the Red Army began to pay its respects to one of its favourite sons, following the death of George Best in a London hospital that afternoon.

As had happened following the death of Sir Matt Busby a number of years previously, Old Trafford soon became a shrine to the wayward Irishman, as flowers, scarves, shirts, photographs and candles covered the pavement and wall facing his old manager's statue.

By a strange quirk of fate, United's first home fixture following George's death was a fourth round Carling Cup tie against West Bromwich Albion, the team he had made his League debut against. It was an evening of emotions, with the club paying its former legendary forward a unique and fitting tribute. The electronic advertising boards around the ground flashed up a continuous message – 'George Best – Manchester United 1963–1974, 470 appearances, 179 goals, 1 genius', as his 1968 European Cup-winning teammates filed onto the pitch, along with members of the current squad, the United directors, Graham Williams, the West Bromwich defender who had marked George on his League debut, and Calum Best, George's son.

As the strains of Don Farden's 'Belfast Boy' echoed around the stadium, Sir Alex Ferguson and West Bromwich Albion manager and former Red legend Bryan Robson walked from the tunnel, ahead of the United and West Bromwich teams, carrying two large wreaths as the players of today faced the players of yesterday on either side of the centre line. Master of Ceremonies for the evening, David Meek, a man who had, as the United correspondent for the *Manchester Evening News*, written thousands upon thousands of words on George, introduced Sir Bobby Charlton. It was often suggested that the two United men did not get on, but there was no hint of such ideas

The Munich plaque.

in the United director's message, 'All of the Manchester United family here in this stadium and all the fans around the world, I would just like to say a big thank you to George Best. You'll never be forgotten.' Following this, Sir Alex and Bryan Robson laid their wreaths alongside a banner made by the supporters stating – 'George – Simply The Best' and seconds later, the stadium fell silent amid the rustle of paper, as the supporters held aloft the colour poster of George that they had been given upon entry into the ground as part of the tribute to the genius.

Today, George is remembered by the imposing statue standing on the Old Trafford forecourt, immortalised alongside his teammates Denis Law and Sir Bobby Charlton, one of the many 'must-see' things for any visitor to the ground.

Turning away from the statue of the 'Trinity' and heading down towards the main entrance to the inner sanctums of the stadium there is the Munich plaque, now in its third home on the stadium walls, with the Munich clock on the stadium wall opposite.

A hundred yards or so further on is the mouth of the Munich Tunnel, created in 2008 for the fiftieth anniversary of the air disaster, when Matt Busby's talent-laden team was cruelly destroyed on its way home from the European Cup tie in Belgrade. It was officially opened following the fiftieth anniversary service held at the ground, by David Gill and Roger Byrne Jnr, son of United's captain at the time of the disaster. They were accompanied by survivors Bobby Charlton, Harry Gregg, Bill Foulkes, Kenny Morgans and Albert Scanlon. The Tunnel is another tribute to those players and officials who lost their lives in the crash, while also telling the story of the rebuilding that followed.

Right: The Munich clock at Manchester United's Old Trafford club.

Below: Panels from the Munich Tunnel.

Above left: The United Trinity: Best, Law and Charlton.

Above right: The statue of Sir Alex Ferguson above the entrance to the museum.

Below: The Sir Alex Ferguson Stand.

The entrance to the United Museum and Stadium Tour.

On Saturday 5 November 2011, prior to United's fixture against Sunderland, Sir Alex Ferguson walked onto the Old Trafford pitch accompanied by the club's chief executive, David Gill, in order to receive a presentation to commemorate his twenty-five years as manager. Unbeknown to the United manager, work had been carried out under the cover of darkness and amid the utmost secrecy, dismantling the words 'Old Trafford Manchester' from the front of the North Stand and replacing them with 'Sir Alex Ferguson Stand'. The work had begun once the final organised tour of the stadium had finished on the Thursday evening and went on until 2 a.m. the following morning, with the six-man team, using abseils to inch down from the roof of the stand, having been asked to sign confidentiality agreements, as had the company that produced the huge red lettering. Only eight club employees knew about the secret and it was a very surprised Sir Alex Ferguson when he was asked to turn around the covers removed from the large red lettering.

Just over a year later, on 23 November 2012, a wet Friday morning in Manchester, a bronze statue of Sir Alex Ferguson was unveiled by the manager's wife Lady Cathy, above the entrance to the United Museum, in the presence of the current first-team squad, numerous former players, club officials and supporters. The statue was the work of Philip Jackson, who was responsible for those of Sir Matt Busby and the 'United Trinity'. 'Normally people die before they see their statue', commented the United manager. 'I'm outliving death!'

Before leaving Old Trafford, and if you have not yet been and intend to go on the Stadium Tour, when you do pause for a few minutes as you either sit in the stand looking down on the pitch, or as you walk around the touchline towards the old tunnel. Think about all those marvellous players who have graced the Old Trafford turf. All of those players, except for the stars of today, are simply mere memories, but two are much closer than you think, as Matt Busby's first post-war captain Johnny Carey and one of the club's greatest goalscorers Dennis Viollet actually had their ashes scattered on the pitch at the Stretford End goal.

Above left: Johnny Carey.

Above right: Denis Viollet.

Left: The Manchester United youth team in 1956, with Bert Whalley far left in the back row.

Carey, an Irishman from Dublin, made his debut in 1937 after joining United from St James Gate, for a fee of £250 and went on to make 344 appearances for the club, captaining the team to FA Cup success in 1948 and the First Division title in 1952. He was also named Footballer of the Year in 1949. Retiring in 1953, he moved into management. Viollet on the other hand was a local lad, living near City's then Maine Road ground. But they failed to act quickly enough and the Manchester Schoolboy was snapped up by United.

Making his debut in 1953, he won championship medals in 1956 and 1957. Surviving the Munich disaster, he went on to break the club goalscoring record, with thirty-two League goals (from thirty-six games) in season 1959/60. He joined Stoke City in January 1962 for a transfer fee of £25,000.

One of the club's unsung heroes, Bert Whalley, also had his ashes scattered over the Old Trafford turf following his funeral service in Trafalgar Square Methodist Church (now West End Methodist), Ashton Under Lyne, and his cremation at Dukinfield Crematorium.

Whalley joined United as a player making thirty-eight appearances over the course of eleven seasons before joining the coaching staff. He was one those unfortunately killed in the Munich air disaster.

Leaving the Munich Tunnel and walking back across the forecourt, where the players used to park their cars on a match day and where Duncan Edwards would tie his bicycle to a roan-pipe with a piece of string (honest), we turn left onto Sir Matt Busby Way. This was formally known as Warwick Road North and was renamed after the former United manager in 1993.

Crossing the railway bridge, past the plaque in memory of James Gibson and the United Foundation building on the corner of Railway Road, one of the row of houses on your right was once the home of United manager John (Jack) Robson, who was in charge of team matters between 1914 and 1921. Robson was actually the first official to take on the mantle of 'manager', as previous holders of this office held the title of 'secretary'. Although he kept United in the First Division, they were blighted by inconsistency and were slipping towards relegation. Ill-health forced Robson to quit his post in October 1921, but he continued as assistant to his replacement, John Chapman. He died in his Railway Road home on 12 January 1922. Jimmy Delaney, the outside right in the 1948 FA Cup-winning side, lived in No. 8.

Making something of a short detour along Railway Road, on the other side of the railway from Old Trafford, No. 68 was the home of another name from United's history – Enoch 'Knocker' West. The robust inside-forward, whose performances across the railway line often made the headlines, was to find himself well and truly in the public eye following the First Division fixture against Liverpool on 2 April 1915.

Right: Sir Matt Busby Way.

Below left: Enoch West.

Below right: Enoch West's former home on Railway Road.

On the morning of the match, FA representatives Mr Fredrick Wall and Mr Arthur Kingscott visited the ground to discuss arrangements for the forthcoming FA Cup final, to be held at the ground on 24 April. It was rather fortunate that they had to leave prior to the start of the game as the events of that particular afternoon produced much debate in the days and weeks ahead.

On a pouring-wet afternoon, the 15,000 crowd had to endure more than adverse weather conditions, with a performance from both teams which produced some very dubious play. United began the game quite promisingly and indeed opened the scoring with a goal from Anderson. Liverpool, however, were expected to take both points, as United were not enjoying the best of seasons, sitting in a precarious position, third-bottom of the League with only eight games remaining and a place in Division Two beckoning.

However, as the first half progressed, the visitors showed little appetite for the game and play sluggishly dragged on to the interval. Half-time opinion suggested that the second forty-five minutes would see the home side up against it, as their Lancashire neighbours committed themselves more to attack and began to show their true form. As it was to turn out, this was not the case and it soon became obvious to a large majority of the crowd that they were witnessing something a little more involved than a simple game of football. Voices of displeasure soon began to echo around the ground.

Play continued to be rather mundane, until a United attack on the visitors' goal saw a Liverpool defender being penalised and a penalty kick being awarded. Much to the crowd's amazement, centre-half O'Connell stepped up to take the spot-kick, instead of the regular penalty-taker Anderson. Seconds later, O'Connell's effort gave the goalkeeper no cause for concern, as it flew well wide of the post.

Anderson eventually did secure the points for United with his second goal, although near the end, Liverpool's Pagnam almost pulled a goal back, but his shot rebounded off the crossbar, when it looked easier to score. For his effort, he received a severe reprimand from some of his teammates, as the crowd looked on in disbelief.

Two valuable points for United, but the press were not lacking in comment on the fixture. 'The most uninteresting game ever seen at the ground', wrote the *Sporting Chronicle* correspondent, while the *Daily Dispatch* reporter penned, 'United's West was clearly employed in the second half in kicking the ball as far out of play as he could.'

A couple of weeks after the match, a letter appeared in the *Sporting Chronicle*, signed 'Football King', on behalf of a firm of bookmakers, asking if anyone could help with information relating to several players betting on the United *v.* Liverpool match ending in a 2-0 win for the home side? This opened a can of worms, and although the finger of suspicion was pointed at several United players, they managed to keep their minds on playing, with relegation being avoided.

In the meantime, a committee was assembled by the Football League to investigate the allegations arising from the match and the referee, John Sharpe, was even quoted as saying that following the penalty incident, he 'suspected that something was amiss', but decided to continue with the game, although it was the most extraordinary match that he had ever officiated over. United manager John Robson was also disgusted by the performances of both teams and had left the ground before the final whistle. Following many hours of questioning players from both sides, the investigating committee announced that four Liverpool players, along with Turnbull, West and Whalley of United were to be suspended *sine die* from football.

Much was made of the case, and 'Knocker' West went to great lengths to declare his innocence in the matter. So incensed was he that he decided to take the matter to court. Prior to a home match during the First World War, he even stood outside Old Trafford, having made the short journey from his home in nearby Railway Road, handing out leaflets which stated that he was prepared to give £50 (quite a sum in those days) to any Red Cross Fund if anyone could prove that he had placed a bet on, or won any money from, the Good Friday fixture. No one ever came forward.

On 5 July 1917, some two years after the eventful confrontation, the court case opened and while some players denied all knowledge of any attempts to fix the outcome of the game, others, including Sheldon of Liverpool (and a former United player) suggested otherwise. It was revealed that on the morning of the match, he had journeyed to Manchester alone, meeting up with his former United teammates Turnbull, Whalley and West in the Dog and Partridge pub close to Old Trafford. After much conversation and debating, it was agreed that the result of the game would be 2-0 to United, with a goal in each half. Sheldon had been approached previously and had made arrangements with some of his Liverpool teammates regarding fixing the result and everything could be finalised. The seeds for the infamous fixed game were sown only a short walk from West's home and indeed, United's Old Trafford home.

If you leave Railway Road and turn into Partridge Street you will come to the Bishop Blaize pub at the corner on your right.

The Bishop Blaize is, many would argue, a United landmark in itself, as a favoured match day watering hole, but a few yards to the left of the main entrance was the site of the meeting place of West and his fellow conspirators, the Dog and Partridge.

The main road opposite the Bishop's is the A56 Chester Road, but before we proceed along to the right, cross at the traffic lights and head down towards the other Old Trafford, the home of Lancashire County Cricket Club.

The second road on the right is Barlow Road, and No. 2 was formerly the digs of Duncan Edwards.

Back up towards Chester Road, cross back over at the lights to find our next stop on the 'United Tour of Manchester'. If walking, remain on the right-hand side of the road, as your destination is a mere ten minutes or so away, but whether walking or driving, look for the Greatstone Hotel on your left. Opposite this you cannot miss the war memorial. There is nothing on the memorial itself, but if you look at the large plaque on the wall behind it and scan the names, you will find, from the East Surrey Regiment, Sgt A. Turnbull. Killed in action during the First World War, at Arras in France on 3 May 1917, Turnbull was United legend, 'Sandy', the man who scored the only goal of the 1909 FA Cup final against Bristol City and United's first goal at their new Old Trafford home the following year.

Ayrshire-born Turnbull was a stocky inside-forward, who began his playing career with Hurlford Thistle, his local club, before moving south to join Manchester City in July 1902. With City, he won a Second Division championship medal in 1903 and an FA Cup winner's medal the following year, before moving across town to join United as part of City's 'mid-season sale', forced upon them when numerous players (including Sandy) were banned by the Football Association due to illegal payments.

Above: The First World War memorial opposite the Greatstone Hotel on Chester Road.

Inset: The details of Sandy Turnbull on the plaque.

Below: The 1909 FA Cup final goal.

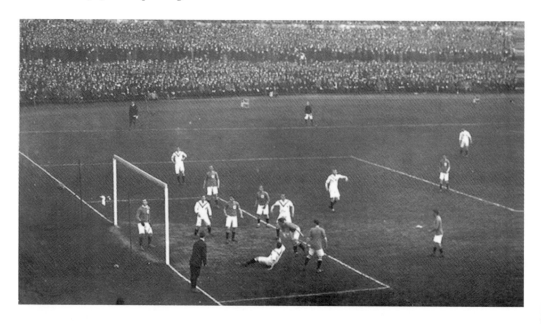

Above left: Walker Crickmer.

Above right: Walter Crickmer's gravestone in Stretford Cemetery.

Proceeding down Chester Road, follow signposts for the A5145 on your left, taking you into Edge Lane. Take the third on the left, into Lime Road, where we come to Stretford Cemetery (M32 8HX), the resting place of Walter Crickmer, United's secretary at the time of Munich. He joined the club as secretary in 1926, but such was his influence and ability that he also served the club as manager, on not one but two separate occasions. The first, in season 1931/32, was when he assisted Louis Rocca, between the reigns of Herbert Bamlett and Scott Duncan; the second, a much lengthier spell, was between 1937 and 1945, following the latter's resignation.

It was during this second period in the Old Trafford manager's office that he played a major part in the setting up of the legendary MUJACs – the forerunner of the youth team set up which would produce so many talented youngsters for the club. Crickmer unfortunately lost his life in the Munich air disaster and his grave can be found on the left, just inside the main gate of the cemetery.

Upon leaving the cemetery, proceed back along Lime Street and head straight across onto Kings Road. Continue along this road until you approach a large roundabout, where you turn left, taking you into Great Stone Road.

Proceeding along here, take the first turning on the left, into Gorse Avenue (M32 0UL), looking for No. 19. This is rather easy to identify, as it has a blue plaque on the wall. The plaque, unveiled on 7 July 2011, identifies that United legend, Duncan Edwards lived here during his time with United.

Born in the West Midlands town of Dudley, Duncan, who signed for United as an England schoolboy international in 1951, is still fondly spoken about today and is considered the greatest England player of his generation, with a golden career in front of him. Having stormed through the United junior sides, capturing the imagination of many with his exploits in the FA Youth Cup, he made his United debut as a sixteen-year-old amateur on 4 April 1953, against Cardiff City at Old Trafford. Two years later, he was pulling on the white of England for the first time against Scotland at Wembley.

Left: Duncan Edwards in action.

Inset: A plaque commemorating Duncan Edwards in Gorse Avenue.

Below left: Tommy Taylor.

Inset: A plaque commemorating Tommy Taylor in Great Stone Road.

Below right: The tribute inside the Quadrant pub to those who lost their lives in Munich.

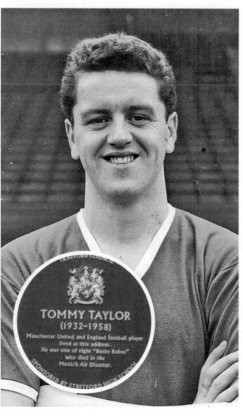

By the age of twenty-one, he had won a further seventeen full England caps, six Football League caps and six under-23 level, to accompany those won at schoolboy and youth level. He also won numerous county honours as a schoolboy, playing under fifteen matches while only eleven. With United, he had three FA Youth Cup winner's medals, two First Division championship medals and a FA Cup runners-up medal.

Despite his build, he was an extremely talented footballer, quick on his feet, while possessing the power to cover every blade of grass on the pitch for ninety minutes. He was also capable of adapting either a defensive or an attacking role. Off the field, however, he was a quiet, shy and unassuming person.

Sadly, injuries received in the Munich air disaster on 6 February 1958 proved to be too much even for Duncan to survive, and he died fifteen days later in the Rechts der Isar hospital in Germany. Had it not been for Munich, there is little doubt among those who knew him and those who had seen him play that he would have led both England and United to countless more honours. Legend is an often-overused word, but it is certainly not in this case.

While parked on Gorse Avenue, you might like to leave your car (or if you are on foot), turn and head back towards Great Stone Road, turning right, and find number 22 (M32 0ZP) identified by another blue plaque, this time identifying the former home of centre-forward Tommy Taylor.

Barnsley-born Taylor began his professional career with his local club, but was out of the game for some eleven months due to a knee injury received while on National Service. Making a complete recovery, he was soon attracting the interest of bigger clubs and it was United who won the race for his signature, with Matt Busby paying out £29,999 (refusing to burden the player with a £30,000 price tag). Arriving at Old Trafford with his boots in a brown paper bag, he soon settled in and was a more-than-capable successor to Jack Rowley. Superb in the air, he was totally unselfish and would drag defenders wide to create opportunities for his teammates. With United, he scored 128 goals in 189 outings, with sixteen in nineteen appearances for England. Like many of his teammates, he lost his life at Munich in 1958.

Heading back down Great Stone Road, as we approach the roundabout you will notice the Quadrant pub (M32 8GR). Inside, there is an excellent tribute (*see illustration opposite*) to all the players, officials, newspapermen and the others who lost their lives at Munich.

After leaving the pub, take the first on the left into Kings Road and look for No. 171 and 233, the former homes of Geoff Bent and Mark Jones respectively.

Geoff Bent was the reserve team full-back who travelled to Belgrade as Roger Byrne's understudy, and would have played in the European Cup tie against Red Star had the United captain failed to recover from an injury he had received in the First Division fixture against Arsenal at Highbury the previous Saturday.

Centre-half Mark Jones, like his teammate Tommy Taylor, was also born in Barnsley and it was as an England schoolboy international that he came to the attention of United, moving to Old Trafford straight from school. Working his way through the junior and reserve sides, he made his United debut against Sheffield Wednesday on 7 October 1953 as a seventeen-year-old. But due to the prolonged career of Allenby Chilton, Jones had to wait patiently to make the number five shirt his own. His breakthrough finally came during season 1954/55 and he never really looked back, becoming a solid cornerstone of the United defence. Had it not been for Munich, there is every possibility that Mark Jones would have been capped by England to add to his list of honours at club level. Although a formidable centre-half, off the field Jones could often be found smoking a pipe and contentedly attending to his budgerigars.

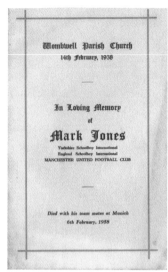

Wombwell Parish Church
14th February, 1958

—

In Loving Memory
of
Mark Jones
Yorkshire Schoolboy International
England Schoolboy International
MANCHESTER UNITED FOOTBALL CLUB

—

Died with his team mates at Munich
6th February, 1958

Above left: Geoff Bent's house today.

Above right: Mark Jones' memorial service cover.

Left: Mark Jones' home today.

Below left: Matt Busby arrives home from hospital after the Munich disaster.

Below right: Matt Busby's former home today.

Continue along Kings Road, which becomes Chorlton Road (B5218) and take the first junction on the right that takes you onto Withington Road. Travel down this road and straight across Wilbraham Road and then take the first on the left into Kings Road (M21 0XY) – a totally different one from before. You are now looking for No. 210, the former home of Sir Matt Busby.

One of the more interesting stories about Busby's former home, or at least the outside of it, occurred one morning while the United manager was sitting enjoying his breakfast. Suddenly, from outside there was a loud crash. His wife Jean immediately dashed to the window and looked out to see what had happened: when she was asked by her husband what had happened, she replied that Roger Byrne had just crashed into the garden wall! Apparently, the car had skidded on some ice on the road. Byrne, the United captain at the time, thankfully was unhurt and his manager gave him a lift to training.

Southern Cemetery

Taking up the trail again, leave Kings Road, turning left into Withington Road just before it becomes Kingsbrook Road. From here, turn right into Mauldeth Road and left onto the A5145 – Barlow Moor Road. Following this, you will come to the Southern Cemetery and the Manchester Crematorium on the left.

Thankfully there is a map of Southern Cemetery, with all the plots and different sections marked out, as without this, you could spend considerable time searching for the various graves in the vast area.

Before venturing into the cemetery itself, we will visit the crematorium, which is conveniently situated alongside. In the remembrance book for February there is a dedication to 'Byrne, Roger William. Born 8 September 1929. Died 6 February 1958. Captain of Manchester United FC and English international.' This is sadly the only memorial to the captain of the Busby Babes. It may well be the only memorial, but the memories of this outstanding full-back still linger on today.

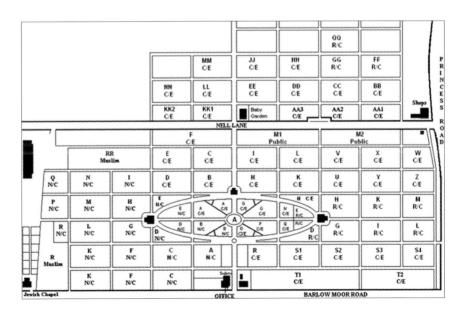

A map of Southern Cemetery.

Roger Byrne was a local lad, born in Gorton, who attended Abbey Hey junior school and Burnage Grammar School. His footballing career began at Ryder Brow Youth Club and it was from here that he joined United. His formative years, however, were not as a defender, but either on the left side of midfield or on the left-wing. An equally talented cricketer, he did his National Service in the RAF, but rather surprisingly failed to make his station football team. His United debut was made at left-back against Liverpool at Anfield on 21 November 1951, but in the final half-dozen games of that championship-winning season he starred at outside-left, scoring seven goals. Despite this success, he felt uncomfortable playing in that forward position – so much so, that he asked for a transfer, which although granted, was never to materialise and he was soon back in his favoured left-back position.

He was a strong-minded but well-liked individual, who had numerous attributes that made him such an outstanding defender, and he was an obvious successor to Allenby Chilton as club captain. He made his England debut in 1954 and went on to play thirty-three consecutive games, while also winning 'B' and Football League international honours. With United, he led them to consecutive First Division titles in 1956 and 1957, as well as the FA Cup final in 1957, but two days short of his twenty-ninth birthday, he was to perish alongside his teammates at Munich.

Roger Byrne's ashes were scattered in the old garden – February section.

The tragedy of Munich is very much in evidence at the crematorium and indeed in Southern Cemetery itself, with a further six individuals remembered. To the centre-right of the flowerbeds can be found an inscription in the memory of Manchester City goalkeeper Frank Swift. The City

Above left and below left: Roger Byrne's funeral at Flixton parish church.

Above right: A page from the crematorium notebook bearing Roger Byrne's name.

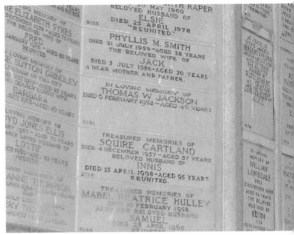

Above left: Frank Swift's plaque at the crematorium.

Above right: Thomas Jackson's plaque at the crematorium.

legend, upon retiring from the game went into journalism and it was in this capacity, working for the *News of the World*, that he had travelled with the United party.

Inside the old building on the wall of the hall can be found a plaque in the memory of the highly respected United correspondent of the *Manchester Evening News*, Tom Jackson, whose name can also be found in the memorial book below that of Roger Byrne. Don Davies, 'Old International' of the *Manchester Guardian*, was also cremated here.

Going back to that memorial book, and above Roger's name, is that of Tom Curry, the United trainer at the time. South Shields born, he began his football career with his local side, Newcastle United, making over 200 appearances between 1919 and 1929 before moving to Stockport County. Spending only one season with County, he retired and began concentrating on the coaching side of the game, taking up the role of trainer with Carlisle United, moving to United, under Scott Duncan, four years later and continuing the role with Matt Busby when football resumed following the Second World War.

Moving now towards Southern Cemetery itself, we will start in the Jewish section, which is beside the main burial area. Interred in this section are Henry Rose (plot CC19), with Willie Satinoff, whose resting place is just on the right-hand side of the path, after you have passed through the gate. Henry Rose was another of the local press corp who followed United around the country and overseas, penning his thoughts and reports for the *Daily Express*. Satinoff, on the other hand, was simply a supporter, a Manchester businessman and a great friend of Matt Busby's, hence his reason for being on board the ill-fated flight. Had he lived, it was expected that he would have soon become a member of the Manchester United board.

Proceeding into the main cemetery, we will first visit the resting place of another member of the press and that of Eric Thompson, known to one and all as 'Sketchbook' and was a reporter with the *Daily Mail* newspaper. Thompson was a noted cartoonist, hence his pen name. The location of Thompson's grave is – N/C B254.

For a number of years countless people walked over an unmarked plot of land in the search for a grave, or as they went to visit that of a loved one, unaware that they were trampling over the final resting place of a footballing legend. A man considered by most to be the game's first 'superstar'. He is one of the few players, if not the only one, to be held in the same affection by supporters of Manchester City and those of Manchester United, which says much for his contribution to the history of both clubs.

His name? Billy Meredith.

Born in Chirk, almost on the Welsh-English border, in 1874, Meredith began work as a miner prior to joining Northwich Victoria as an amateur in 1892, having played with local side Black Park for the previous couple of years. He signed professional with the Vic's in 1893, but soon came to the attention of Manchester City, joining for them in October 1894. With City, he was to win Division Two championship medals in 1899 and 1903 and a FA Cup winner's medal in 1904. However, his reputation was to take something of a dent the following year, when he was accused of attempting to bribe Aston Villa's Alec Leake by offering £10 to throw a game, for which he was suspended until the end of April 1906. At this time City were under investigation by the Football Association for financial irregularities and a number of their players were also suspended.

The accusations against Meredith, and indeed three of his teammates – Sandy Turnbull, Hergert Burgess and Jimmy Bannister – were of little concern to United and all four were duly signed. Meredith made his United debut on New Year's Day 1907, beginning a career with the club that produced First Division championship medals in 1908 and 1911 and another FA Cup winners medal in 1909. There were also two FA Charity Shield successes.

Legend has it that he could be seen meandering down the touchline with a toothpick stuck firmly in his mouth, but he was a tremendously skilful individual, whose ability and accuracy with the ball produced countless goals for his fellow teammates. United gave him a free transfer at the age of forty-seven, having made just over three hundred and thirty appearances, scoring thirty-five goals. When many would have long since retired, he re-signed for City, where he continued to play for a further three years, making his last appearance against Newcastle United in the 1924 FA Cup semi-final at the age of forty-nine and 245 days. With City, he made a total of 390 appearances, scoring 150 goals.

Lying in an unpretentious grave, just as he would have wanted, a throw-in away from that of the Welsh genius, is the grave of the man who laid the foundations for the modern day Manchester United – Sir Matt Busby.

The grave, which can be found in plot G997, is regularly visited by Manchester United supporters, so do not be surprised upon your visit if you are not the only person in the vicinity.

Busby, born in 1909, hailed from Orbiston, near Bellshill in Lanarkshire, a mining community, and as a fifteen-year-old left school, having made the ten-mile round trip on a daily basis to take up a similar employment to his father down the mine. His meagre £2 per week wages made a difference to the family income, but a German's bullet during the Battle of the Somme, robbed the family of its head and biggest money earner, placing a heavy weight on young Matt's shoulders.

With the future looking far from rosy, his mother decided to emigrate to the United States, an idea that Matt, although working full-time down the mines, readily went along with. By now, the football-mad teenager was turning out on a regular basis for Denny Hibernian, and when a scout from Manchester City took a liking to the eighteen year old, the family plans turned on their head.

Had the documentation required to begin a new life across the Atlantic Ocean not taken around nine months to process, then things may well have been different, but with City arriving on the

Above left: William Satinoff's grave.

Above middle: Henry Rose's grave.

Above right: Billy Meredith's grave.

Below: Eric 'Sketchbook' Thomson's grave.

family doorstep, offering the promising footballer a one year, £5 per week contract in February 1928, he managed to persuade his mother to postpone the planned departure for that year and to allow him to fulfil his dreams as a professional footballer. At the end of the twelve months, Busby decided that his immediate future lay in Manchester and all thoughts of emigration were brushed aside.

On 2 November 1929, he made his debut for City in a First Division fixture against Middlesbrough at Maine Road and went on to make a further eleven appearances that season as an inside forward, scoring five goals. His undoubted talent had been noticed by City's cross-town rivals United, bringing an enquiry as to his availability, but little more, as they could not afford the asked-for £150 transfer fee. Busby was not considered inside-forward material, but fortunately the City manager of the time, Peter Hodge, decided to move him back into the half-back line to see if this would improve the player's contribution to the team and his own standard of play.

Fortunately, for both Busby and his manager, the move worked and he went on to create a name for himself as a forceful, intelligent and creative half-back, winning his solitary Scotland cap in 1933 against Wales at Ninian Park, Cardiff. 1934 saw him win an FA Cup winner's medal, having appeared in semi-final losses the previous two seasons, but the following season, 1934/35, he lost his place in City's staring line-up, and despite having made over 200 appearances for the Maine Road side, decided to move across Lancashire and join Liverpool in March 1936, with a fee of £8,000 changing hands.

Before long, Busby was Liverpool's captain, making up a formidable half-back trio with McDougall and Bradshaw, still considered today as Anfield's best ever. Like many footballers, the Second World War played havoc with their careers, but despite the hostilities and having signed up for his National Service with the King's Liverpool Regiment, Busby continued to play, turning out for the likes of Chelsea, Middlesbrough, Reading, Bournemouth, Brentford and Hibs. He was also to make a further seven appearances for Scotland in wartime internationals as well as a Scottish League XI appearance.

When the war ended, Liverpool were keen to make Busby their manager, but following talks with the Anfield board, his gut instinct was to look elsewhere. Back in Manchester, United were looking for a new manager as secretary Walter Crickmer had been running the show and during one of the regular board meetings, Busby's name was mentioned by United's jack-of-all-trades, Louis Rocca, who said that he would write to his friend and see what his immediate plans were. The letter was received and contact made, with a meeting arranged at the club's temporary offices at Cornbrook Cold Storage, premises owned by Chairman James Gibson. Both parties were suitably impressed by each other, terms were agreed and Matt Busby became the new manager of Manchester United.

Requiring a right-hand man, Busby remembered listening to a fellow soldier talking about football while abroad and sought out Welshman Jimmy Murphy, who readily agreed to join him at a bomb-wrecked Old Trafford.

Runners-up in the First Division in the first three immediate post-war seasons, 1946/47, 1947/48 and 1948/49 (a vast improvement on fourteenth in 1938/39) cemented the foundations of a prosperous relationship. It blossomed even more when the FA Cup was won in 1948, with United defeating Blackpool 4-2 at Wembley in a ninety minutes still considered one of the best under the old twin towers. Building on this success, Busby finally clinched the First Division title at the end of season 1951/52, but despite this, continued to keep one eye on the future, having decided that his ageing players would soon need to be replaced, and placing the emphasis on a youth system that would become the envy of every club in the country.

Above: Liverpool *v.* Manchester United programme, showing Busby playing for Liverpool.

Right: Matt Busby as a player.

His vision was spot on and his ambitions fulfilled when, one by one, his teenage recruits (David Pegg, Jackie Blanchflower, Denis Viollet, Eddie Colman, Duncan Edwards and the likes) coupled with the occasional purchase (Johnny Berry and Tommy Taylor), developed into a swashbuckling attacking force that brought crowds clicking through the turnstiles wanting see for themselves Busby's 'Babes'. They were First Division champions in 1955/56 and again in 1956/57. They were denied the FA Cup in 1957 only due to an injury to goalkeeper Ray Wood that left them with ten men for a considerable part of the game. The world was their oyster.

The European Cup had been introduced in 1956, but the Football League denied League champions Chelsea from entering. A letter forbidding United from entering the 1956/57 competition was sent to Old Trafford, but Busby was having none of it. Europe in Busby's opinion was where they should be. The European Cup was the way ahead and United were entering and no one would stop them.

Although it was a journey into the unknown, with pre- and end-of-season fixtures against foreign opposition the usual fare, United took the competition by the scruff of the neck, hammering twelve past the Belgians of Anderlecht over two legs, without reply. Defeating Borussia Dortmund 3-2 on aggregate, which was followed by arguably Manchester United's greatest team performance to date, a 3-0 victory over Athletico Bilbao at Maine Road (there were no floodlights as yet at Old Trafford), to go through 6-5 on aggregate.

Unfortunately, the semi-final draw paired United with a Real Madrid team who were undoubtedly the best in Europe, and having lost 3-1 in Madrid, they could not turn the match around back in Manchester, where the Spaniards fought out a competitive 2-2 draw.

A 1948 team group photograph, including Matt Busby.

The following season, United were back in the competition and Busby felt that this time, his team could go all the way, having learnt much from the previous campaign. Shamrock Rovers, Dukla Prague and Red Star Belgrade were all easily dealt with, with AC Milan lying in wait as Busby and his players left Belgrade following the 3-3 draw that gave them a 5-4 passage into the semi-finals for the second consecutive season.

It was a game that many would not play in, as following a refuelling stop at Munich, the BEA Elizabethan aircraft crashed on its third attempt at take-off, killing twenty-three of the forty-four people on board, all but three instantly: a total that included eight United players. Busby was, himself, near to death with multiple injuries, but over the days and weeks ahead, miraculously pulled through and returned home to see the rebuilt United, under the guidance of Jimmy Murphy, who had missed the game in Belgrade due to international commitments with Wales, lose 2-0 to Bolton Wanderers in the FA Cup final.

Slowly returning to fitness, Busby and Murphy continued the rebuilding work and, having just managed to avoid relegation to the Second Division, took United to Wembley in 1963, where the new recruits to the cause (Denis Law and Pat Crerand) played a major part in the 3-1 defeat of favourites Leicester City. This was the springboard to success and the First Division title was won in seasons 1964/65 and 1966/67 with Munich survivor Bobby Charlton, alongside the two previously mentioned Scots and a youngster by the name of George Best, once again making Manchester United the team that everyone wanted to see – and beat.

An injury to Best more or less robbed United of a European Cup final place in 1966 and it was beginning to look as if Busby's dream of capturing the trophy was slowly fading from view. The

The 1957 team.

1967/68 competition was viewed by many as his last chance and victories over Hibernians of Malta, Sarajevo and Gornik Zabre took them into the semi-finals once again. Lying in wait were old foes Real Madrid, not the team of old, but still formidable opponents. A solitary 1-0 victory at Old Trafford in the first leg was considered not enough to take United into the final, and with Real leading 3-1 in the second leg, with fifteen minutes to go, it looked like United were once again so near, but so far.

Foulkes headed on a Crerand free-kick, Sadler forced the ball over the line and then completely out of the blue, Best centred the ball more in hope than anything else and by some manner of means centre-half and Munich survivor Bill Foulkes appeared from nowhere to equalise. It was a goal that would send United into the Wembley final.

Under the twin towers, on the evening of 29 May 1968, Benfica took United to extra-time, or perhaps that should read Alex Stepney did, with a point-blank save from the usually cynical Eusebio, with the game balanced at 1-1. In that additional thirty minutes, however, United stormed past the Portuguese, scoring thrice to bring Busby the biggest accolade in club football. Following that success, it was no longer simply Matt Busby, but *Sir* Matt Busby – but his days at the helm at Old Trafford were numbered.

A year later, he retired, handing over the reins to Wilf McGuinness, but the job proved too much for the untried manager, and in December 1970 he was back in charge for the remainder of season 1970/71 until the appointment of Frank O'Farrell. He continued as a director until 1982, when he was made club president was awarded a testimonial match in August 1991. With Alex Ferguson as manager of his beloved United, he longed for the club to win the championship

NIGHT FINAL

Morris · Austin · Wolseley
Riley – M.G.
Consult the
B.M.C. Retail Dealers
E.E.Brown: Co
(Smethwick) Ltd.
ST. PAUL'S ROAD, SMETHWICK
SME 1138 – 9

Evening Despatch

2¼d.   No. 20,746   BIRMINGHAM   Thursday, February 6, 1958

MANCHESTER UTD. PLANE CRASHES: 28 DEAD

Numbing blow...

A CHARTERED AIRLINER CARRYING THE MAN-
CHESTER UNITED FOOTBALL TEAM HOME FROM
BELGRADE CRASHED SHORTLY AFTER TAKE-OFF
FROM MUNICH TODAY.

Reports from Munich said that 28 of the 40 people on board were
killed when the plane crashed into houses and exploded.

TODAY, British football with its millions of followers is plunged into deepest possible mourning, writes DICK KNIGHT. The sport has lost many of its most brilliant performers, belonging to a club which after uncertain post-war years had helped to put our football firmly on the map. The big football centres of the country have their own pets and fancies, but the exploits of Manchester United have attracted unanimous praise. I say this. No soccer fan in the

suppose you can have crashes just as easily travelling by rail or road." Aston Villa manager Eric Houghton said: "I was afraid this would happen one of these days. That is why we never flew to Paris during the close season." Mr. J. Howley, of Wolves, said: "It is the greatest shock I have ever had in football. Obviously, I do not know it

will affect our match at Old Trafford on Saturday." George Noakes, Wolves chief scout: "This is the greatest shock I have ever had, Manchester United are our greatest rivals. But this has knocked the bottom out of all of us at Wolverhampton." Vic Buckingham, West Bromwich Albion manager: "It's just ghastly. What more can anyone say!"

The *Evening Despatch* announces the Munich disaster.

again and with twenty-six years having passed since the last title, he was as happy as any other supporter when United won the Premier League in 1993.

Manchester United had by now come the full cycle. Ferguson had taken over a team in disarray and, like Busby, had rebuilt it, creating a United side that played football the proper way. It was therefore, as if Sir Matt knew his club, the one that had saw him build not one but three great teams, was now in more-than-capable hands, when he passed away on the evening of 20 January 1994 in the Alexandra Hospital in Cheadle.

Thousands lined the route as his coffin left St John's Roman Catholic church in High Lane Chorlton, proceeding to Old Trafford before making its way to his final resting place in Southern Cemetery.

With Sir Matt Busby being rightly acclaimed as the man whose foresight and managerial ability laid the foundations of the Manchester United that we have today, not far from the grave of the genial Scot is that of another man for whom Manchester United will be eternally grateful and without whose intervention, there is every possibility that there would be no Manchester United Football Club. That man was John Henry Davies and more can be read about him in the 'Miscellaneous' section of this book. The Davies family grave can be found at plot 'B36' in the 'Non-conformist section'.

Public Transport details to Southern Cemetery: Nearest Train Station – East Didsbury. Bus Service – Barlow Moor Road. Metrolink Station – Stretford.

Above: United win the European Cup, 1968.

Below left: Matt Busby.

Below right: Matt Busby's grave.

Miscellany

Should you have developed a thirst for everything United, or indeed had one in the first place, there are a number of other places that you may wish to visit, although some may have altered greatly, or indeed disappeared from view altogether since the days when they could be considered part of Manchester United history.

From his shop on Ashton New Road the former United captain Charlie Roberts sold his own 'Duckrobell' tobacco blend, named after himself and his teammates Alec Bell and Dick Duckworth! The original buildings are long gone but parts of it, including a plaque commemorating Roberts were reused in the current buildings. No. 591 Ashton New Road (the address of Robert's shop) is, at the time of writing, a Chinese takeaway.

Another notable club captain and one, who above all others did much to keep Newton Heath alive and indeed secure the future of the club that we have today was Harry Stafford. His part in United's history has been documented elsewhere in this book, but one item of note relating to his 200-game career for the club was, when gifted a benefit match, he choose to play at night, under Wells lights, with a gilded ball. On the night of the match there was a strong wind, and no sooner had one light been relit, when another went out. The match was brought to a premature end by the referee and it was then found that many players were already in the warmth of the dressing rooms!

The Bridge Inn pub on the corner of Beswick Street and Mill Street was run by Harry Stafford while he was captain of Newton Heath, prior to his taking over the Imperial Hotel on Piccadilly.

St Luke's Church, Dukinfield

Situated in east Manchester, on Kings Street, Dukinfield, SK16 4NQ, is St Luke's church, where there is an illuminated parchment, framed and standing on a side table. It names the dead and the survivors of the Air Disaster at Munich on 6 February 1958.

George Best

Detailing all the places in Manchester associated with the legendary George Best would more or less take up a book on its own, and even then some of his old haunts would be missed out as no one knew where the wayward Irishman was half the time. Here, we will simply deal with the places that crop up most frequently in the George Best story.

We kick off our mini-tour of Manchester in the wake of Belfast the genius at the house he called 'home' when he first arrived in a strange and certainly daunting city. This was at No. 9 Aycliffe Avenue in Chorlton-cum-Hardy (M21 7WJ), a short distance from the previously mentioned Southern Cemetery. This was the home of Mrs Fullaway. George arrived here with fellow Irishman Eric McMordie in July 1961, but only spent one night here before the pair made their way back home. Much to United's eternal relief, George returned, settled down and went on to become one of football's greatest players.

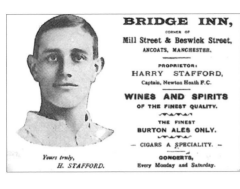

BRIDGE INN,
CORNER OF
Mill Street & Beswick Street,
ANCOATS, MANCHESTER.

PROPRIETOR:
HARRY STAFFORD,
Captain, Newton Heath F.C.

WINES AND SPIRITS
OF THE FINEST QUALITY.

THE FINEST
BURTON ALES ONLY.

— CIGARS A SPECIALITY. —

CONCERTS,
Every Monday and Saturday.

Yours truly,
H. STAFFORD.

Above: The Bridge Inn, proprietor
Harry Stafford.

Right: Charlie Roberts' newsagent
and tobacconist.

Below: St Luke's church, Dukinfield.

George remained under Mrs Fullaway's roof until 1969, when he felt it was time to have a home of his own, and he was perhaps ill-advised to have a £30,000 house built in Bramhall, which was certainly a far cry from downtown Chorlton. His new fashionable abode had a sunken bath, snooker room and a television that appeared from down a chimney. The house soon became something of a goldfish bowl and George was often 'away' from home. Strangely, however, he did allow members of his 'fan club', who won a competition, to spend a couple of nights there. There is certainly no possibility of any of the current United stars allowing such a thing to happen...

As the sixties began to swing, George could certainly be found well to the fore, as life, fashion and of course football began to change. The hair became longer, the fashion more flamboyant, the girlfriends more glamorous, and soon George was the player everyone wanted to see. The turnstiles clicking merrily as the 'Belfast Boy' quickly became the best in the business.

George Best.

On the fashion side of things, he opened his first boutique in Cross Street, Sale moved into a business partnership with Manchester City's Mike Summerbee, opening the Edwardia boutique on Bridge Street in the late sixties. The former shop is now one of the 650 Starbucks coffee shops in the city.

Following ninety minutes of exertion out on the pitch and once the sweat and dirt had been showered off, it was time to hit the town, where the doors of the various nightspots were always open. Having George Best among your Saturday night crowd was certainly good for your business.

George soon clicked that there was money to be made in nightclubs, as well as the other obvious attraction, and before long he had a share in two – Slack Alice, just off Deansgate in Bootle Street, now called 42nd Street, and Oscar's in Cooper Street, a short walk from St Peter's Square. This is now called Tiger Lounge. Blinkers nightclub in King Street was another popular haunt of the United superstar, and for a while he ran their women's football team.

The final featured premises constantly mentioned in the same breath as George, is the (in)famous Brown Bull public house, or (as Sir Matt would often refer to it) the Black Cow! Situated at 187–189 Chapel Street, near to Salford Central station, it is now called Copperheads, and it was at one time the regular haunt of not just George Best, but numerous other local footballers, as well as stars of stage screen and television.

George sadly died on 25 November 2005, aged only fifty-nine, as a result of a lung infection and multiple organ failure. His funeral, held at Stormont, Belfast, on 3 December, was something of a state affair, with thousands lining the streets. He was later buried in Roselawn Cemetery, Ballygowan Road, Crossnacreevy, Belfast, BT5 7UD, His grave is No. 295 in section S. The Best family home can be found at 16 Burren Way, on the Cregagh estate, BT6 0DW, which was purchased by 'Landmark East' in 2011 and is now a holiday rental property. Inside, there are numerous items of memorabilia relating to the United legend.

ADMISSION FREE EVERY NIGHT TO DINERS (INC. SATURDAY)

BLINKERS Restaurant Club

Courtlets House,
38 King Street, West
Manchester M3 2WZ
Telephone: 061-834 5536

Dress: *JACKET & TIE*
(No Denims)

Member's Name

....

LIFE MEMBERSHIP
Member's Signature

....

Restaurant opens 8.30 p.m.
Bars licensed until 2.00 a.m.
except Sunday until 11.30 p.m.

FREE ADMISSION TO MEMBER & GUESTS
ANY NIGHT EXCEPT SATURDAY

Admission ticket to Blinkers nightspot.

Above: George Best's home in Bramhall, Cheshire.

Below: No. 9 Aycliffe Avenue, Chortlton-cum-Hardy, Manchester.

Above left: The Brown Bull public house.

Above right: The entrance to Oscars nightspot.

Below left: George Best.

Below right: George Best's grave site in Roselawn Cemetery, Belfast.

Above: Albert Scanlon's resting place in Agecroft Cemetery.

Left: Albert Scanlon.

Albert Scanlon

Scanlon was one of the Munich survivors, but following the crash, his career would never attain the same heights that he had experienced in the weeks and months prior to that fateful Thursday in February 1958. Had it not been for Munich then there was every possibility that full England honours would have come his way. In later years, life was hard for the one-time Babe, but he was never forgotten by the Old Trafford faithful. Albert is buried in Agecroft Cemetery (M27 8SS).

Maine Road

The former home of Manchester City was not simply a venue visited once a season when both clubs were in the same division of the Football League, or on occasion a neutral ground selected as an the FA Cup semi-final venue when United had progressed that far. It was for a period of time 'home' to Matt Busby's team.

Following bomb damage to Old Trafford on 22 December 1940 during an air raid on nearby Trafford Park and again on 11 March 1941, when the Main Stand (the South Stand today) was destroyed, United were left virtually homeless. The day-to-day running of the club was transferred to Cornbrook Cold Storage, owned by United chairman James W. Gibson, but it was neighbours

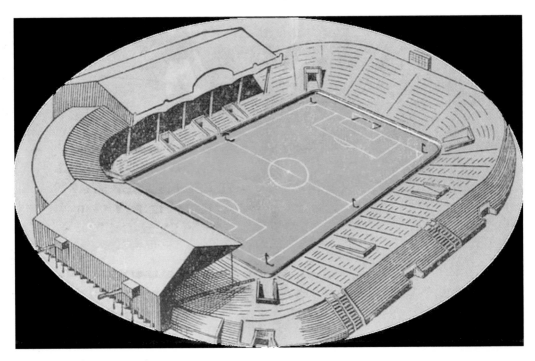

A drawing of Maine Road.

City who came to the rescue with a match day venue, offering their Maine Road ground as a temporary home. Negotiations were quickly carried out and an agreement was reached, with United paying £5,000 a year plus a percentage of the gate receipts. The latter, being an excellent clause in the contract, as attendances were booming, with United in fact attracting a Football League record of 83,260 for their fixture against Arsenal on 17 January 1948.

United returned home for the opening fixture of season 1949/50 against Bolton Wanderers on 24 August, but seven years later had once again to make the cross city move in order to fulfill a couple of fixtures.

Having won the First Division championship in 1955/56, they were invited to participate in the following season's European Cup competition. The competition, introduced twelve months previously, was for the League champions of various European countries, but the Football League had prevented Chelsea, First Division champions for 1954/55, from entering and had attempted to do the same with United. Matt Busby, however, would have none of it, and backed by the Football Association, took United into the European Cup for the first time. The only minor problem was the lack of floodlights at Old Trafford, the construction of which were on the board's agenda, so it was back across town to Manchester City to ask for the use of their Maine Road ground.

Under the City floodlights, United began their European Cup career with an emphatic 10-0 trouncing of Belgian side Anderlecht. This was followed by a more closely fought 3-2 encounter against the German side Borussia Dortmund. It was in the next round, against the Spaniards from Bilbao, that United really came to the fore, in what was perhaps the finest ninety minutes of football played on the Maine Road ground.

Having lost the first leg 5-3, on a snow and slush covered pitch in a not-so-sunny Spain, many thought that United had come to the end of their inaugural season in the European Cup, but goals from Johnny Berry, Tommy Taylor and Denis Viollet gave United a 3-0 victory in a game still spoken about today by those who witnessed it.

Maine Road today is no more, with the Moss Side ground now demolished, and City playing their final match there on 11 May 2003, before their move to what was then called the City of Manchester Stadium.

Carrington

It is certainly a far cry from the old training ground at The Cliff, or indeed the area behind the Stretford End at Old Trafford where impromptu five-a-sides would take place, when life and limbs were put in danger. But where there was easy access to The Cliff, with no fences or hedges and no overzealous security staff around Old Trafford, your only hope of gaining entry into what is known as the Trafford Training Centre or (by the time you read this) the AON Training Complex, is to visit on a Saturday morning when there is a United Academy game on.

Okay, you will not see the inner sanctums, but it will be as close as you get, unless you have the chance of signing for United, or know someone who works there. United Supporters Clubs are sometimes given the opportunity to go and watch the players train, but you are kept well away from the action and even those organised events can be cancelled at very short notice. On an Academy match day you can gain access to one of the buildings, where they serve tea and biscuits free and you can see the superb indoor training facilities for the youngsters, but that is it. The address of the complex is: Birch Road, off Isherwood Road, Carrington, M31 4BH.

Above left: The Carrington main gymnasium.

Above right: The Carrington first-team dressing room.

Above: Carrington from the air.

Below: Carrington main entrance.

Roger Byrne

Roger Byrne was everything that a captain of a football team should be – a player who led by example on the field and had the respect of all his teammates. It would be impossible to include all the birthplaces of all the local players in this book, but due to his standing in the club's history, Roger is included. He was born at No. 13 Beech Street, Gorton, which you will not find on any map today, as it is now called Wistaria Road. He was later to live at No. 20 Edale Avenue, Flixton.

Left: Roger Byrne's birthplace at 13 Beech Street, Gorton, Manchester.

Below: Byrne leads out his young United team at Highbury for a fixture against Arsenal on 1 February 1958. It was to be the last game that he and seven of his teammates would play on English soil.

Moorside High School

Situated on the A580 East Lancs Road, Moorside High School's entry into the pages of this book is due to one of its former pupils, the most decorated footballer of all time – Ryan Joseph Giggs OBE.

   While a pupil at Moorside, he was, however, known to staff and classmates as Ryan Wilson, the change in name coming after his parents split up and he took on the surname of his mother. Ryan Giggs was initially on schoolboy forms with Manchester City, but was snapped up by United, signing professional as a seventeen-year-old in 1990. After progressing through the junior sides, he was given his first-team debut against Everton on 2 March 1991 and went on to become the club's record appearance holder, while season 2012/13 saw him make his thousandth senior career appearance, which included those for United, Wales and Great Britain at Olympic level.

Above: Moorside High School.

Inset: Ryan Giggs was given the Freedom of the City of Salford.

Ryan Giggs' former home on Worsley Road.

Louis Rocca

Luigi Rocca moved from the Italian village of Borzonasca, which lies 22 miles east of Genoa, to the Ancoats area of Manchester in 1865, due to the political and economic unrest in Italy at that time.

After marrying an Italian girl who lived in Sheffield, the couple moved to a small terraced house at No. 64 Rochdale Road, where, in the cellar, they began what was to become a thriving ice-cream business.

Luigi Jnr was born in 1883 and was soon known to one and all as 'Louis', especially around the vicinity of Bank Street Clayton, attracted there through his love of football. At the age of twelve, he became the unofficial 'tea-boy' of Newton Heath Football Club, progressing to looking after the team strips and assisting the grounds man in his duties. From then on, Rocca's involvement with the club became the stuff of legend, with many of his tales becoming clouded as the years passed by.

Recalling his early days at the club, he mentions that he was the person who stood up and suggested the name 'Manchester United' in those grim days when the future of Newton Heath lay in the balance. There is no documented evidence to confirm this, although some sources actually dismiss his claims, with *The Lancashire Courier, The Manchester Evening News* and *The Manchester Guardian*, all who had reporters at the meeting, stating quite clearly:

> Before the meeting broke up, one old supporter suggested that the name of the club should be changed to 'Manchester United', but this did not meet with much favour.

Rocca was only eighteen years of age at the time of those meetings so he could never have been classed as an 'old supporter'. Even his involvement in the story of Harry Stafford's St Bernard's dog is one of three different version that circulate today.

But no matter what, Louis Rocca was certainly very involved with Newton Heath and Manchester United Football Club's. In 1907, he was named chief scout, and it was a post that he held until his death in 1950, with one of his much chronicled transfer dealings being the signing of a young Stockport player by the name of Hugh McLenahan. The player was reportedly unhappy at Stockport and with County planning a fundraising bazaar, the ever-alert Rocca 'donated' three freezers of ice cream to the football club and the transfer of McLenahan was then a foregone conclusion.

Rocca was also instrumental in bringing Matt Busby to the club, along with backroom staff members Tom Curry and Bill Inglis.

Rocca was certainly a man who kept his ear to the ground and always 'knew a man, who knew a man, who could', or had heard where the next schoolboy football prodigy would be playing. Together with his staunch ally and partner Walter Crickmer, and also Mr Gibson, between them they were responsible for laying the foundations that would help Sir Matt Busby and Jimmy Murphy to weave their magic, and also helped to put the club on a firm financial base. Louis Rocca passed away in hospital in 1950 at the age of sixty-seven. After a requiem Mass at his old church, St Anne's, which is in Ancoats, he was buried in St Joseph's Roman Catholic Cemetery, which is in Moston (M40 9QL). Many United staff, players, former players (including Billy Meredith), and fans were in attendance. As he was finally laid to rest, a piece of turf cut from the Old Trafford playing surface was placed upon his coffin.

Right: Louis Rocca's resting place in St Joseph's Roman Catholic Cemetery, Moston, Manchester.

Inset: Louis Rocca.

John Henry Davies, 1864–1927

The name of John Henry Davies cannot be found in any of the statistical records relating to either Manchester United or Newton Heath, as at no time did he ever pull on their famous shirt. But he is, however, one of two men (the other being James W. Gibson) who at different times played such a huge part in Manchester United's history. Through their generosity, and business acumen during difficult periods when some financial injections were required, they prevented the club from becoming extinct.

Davies, born in Cheadle in 1864, did not come from a wealthy family and initially worked as an estate agent and innkeeper. He first moved into the brewing business in the late 1890s as a director of John Henry Lees Brewery in Moss Side (established in 1897), but by the beginning of the next century, he had moved on to become chairman of the Walker & Homfray Brewery. (The company has wrongly been called in United histories 'Walker and Humphries' and 'Walker and Pomfrey'. Both of these are *wrong*. It was as stated 'Walker and Homfrays' and was Salford based.) When it came down to business, he had a keen eye for turning a profit, and was certainly no pushover.

He married into the well-known and very wealthy Tate family, as his wife was Amy Catterall, the niece and ward of Sir Henry Tate, who was a sugar refiner and had established his business in Liverpool in 1869. Henry Tate opened another sugar-refining company in Silvertown in the East End of London, and later used some of his fortune to establish the now famous Tate Gallery in 1897. He had a main business rival at that time named Abram Lyle, who was a cooper and ship owner. Lyle was originally from Greenock in Scotland and had also acquired an interest in a sugar refinery that he later moved to Plaistow Wharf in Silvertown and the two men became bitter rivals. They never met, and it was only after they had both died that the two companies were merged in 1921 to form the Tate & Lyle Sugar Company.

From day one, Henry Tate made it clear to Davies that he was unwelcome in his family, but despite her guardian's disapproval, Amy decided to marry Davies and the couple went on to enjoy a long and happy marriage.

That part of John H. Davies' life story is perfectly straightforward; however, the same certainly cannot be said for how he became involved in Newton Heath and the Manchester United story. One account, the one that is commonly used to relate the tale is as follows.

In late February and early March 1901, Newton Heath Football Club held a fundraising bazaar in the St James Hall, in Oxford Street, Manchester. Harry Stafford, who was the club captain, had been in attendance each day and had worked tirelessly on the club's behalf in an effort to raise as much money as possible. Stafford owned a St Bernard's dog and had it with him each day in the hall, but on the last afternoon of the bazaar the dog, with a collection tin around his neck, wandered out and away from the hall. It wandered into a pub across the road named the Oxford Arms that at that time was managed by a Mr Thomas, but owned by John Henry Davies' company.

Mr Thomas kept the dog for a few days, and when John Henry visited the establishment, he showed the dog to him. He was quite taken by the beautiful St Bernard and began making enquiries as to who its owner could be and eventually, those enquiries led him to Harry Stafford.

By this time, Davies, and more to the point, his daughter, had developed a strong liking for the dog and wished to keep it so that he could present it to his daughter on her birthday. Upon meeting Stafford, he negotiated the purchase of the dog, but that meeting began a strong, unbreakable friendship. Just days later, Harry Stafford was installed as the licensee of the Bridge Inn, which used to stand on the corner of Old Mill Street and Beswick Street, in the Bradford area of Manchester.

Twelve months later, Newton Heath Football Club was on the verge of extinction and had already been issued with a winding-up order. A supporters' meeting was called and was held at the New Islington Public Hall on Tuesday 18 March 1902 to discuss if the club had any future.

On the night of the meeting, a boisterous crowd packed the hall and a very noisy meeting ensued. When the financial predicament of the club was read out, Harry Stafford stood up and told the onlookers that he knew of four other men beside himself who were willing to put in sums of money to help stabilise, and keep the club afloat financially. One of those four men was John Henry Davies.

In hindsight, it was no surprise really, as both he and his wife had become well-known philanthropists who were noted for their support of local sports in the Manchester area. At a meeting at the same hall just four weeks later, the name of Newton Heath was changed to Manchester United, and Davies was installed as chairman, a position that he would keep until his death in 1927.

Now, however, there is a very different angle to the involvement of Davies and one that might be nearer to the actual truth. George Lawton was an accountant at the Walker & Homfray's brewery, who used to lock up the offices on a Saturday afternoon and cycle over to Newton Heath to watch the local side in action. He was a very loyal supporter, cycling to every game no matter the weather and through time, became very friendly with club captain Harry Stafford.

One Saturday afternoon, he was cycling towards the old ground on Oldham Road as usual, when he was knocked off his bicycle by a horse and trap. Picking himself up and preparing to voice his opinion of the driver, he had to bite his tongue, as it was none other than his boss, John Henry Davies, heading home from a late lunch.

Davies duly inquired as to where his employee was in such a hurry to get to and he was surprised to find out that it was to watch a game of football and was enlightened to the briefest of details relating to Newton Heath before his accountant dashed off to the game.

When Lawton arrived at the ground, he was shocked to discover that the bailiffs were also in attendance, standing alongside the three turnstiles and taking the money as it was paid by the supporters to enter the ground. Following the game, he discussed the situation with Stafford and together, they set off for his employer's home and managed to persuade his boss to visit the depleted ground, which was without any cover, causing low attendances on wintry afternoons. Confessing that he had never seen a football match, he decided to pay off all existing debts and was soon attending games on a regular basis. Lawton later became a director of the club.

Perhaps the 'dog story' sounded better, but unfortunately there is no one alive to ask. But no matter what version is true, J. H. Davies did put money into the club and arguably saved it from extinction. During his tenure at the club it was not unknown that he would make sure that local charities were supported, particularly by donating the gate receipts from public practice matches, with the amount taken at the gate being with matched with same amount from his own pocket.

Under his charge, Manchester United enjoyed their very first halcyon years of success, and it was his foresight that enabled the club to move to Old Trafford. Once again he showed his

Left: The tombstone of John Henry Davies in Southern Cemetery, Manchester.

Inset: J. H. Davies.

business acumen. The land upon which the new ground was to be built was owned by the Manchester Brewery Company, a company that he owned. The Brewery Company then leased the land back to Manchester United Football Club. In 1894, the Manchester Ship Canal had opened and the inland port of Manchester lay just a short distance away from the land where the new stadium would eventually be. In 1896, a consortium named the Trafford Park Syndicate bought land from Sir Humphrey de Trafford, which lay to the north west of the place where the stadium would be. This area in later years would become known as Trafford Park and became the largest industrial estate in Europe, which attracted some of the largest manufacturing companies in the world to build their plants there.

The area became a hive of industry with the close proximity of the docks being crucial to the local trade and industry, and the arrival of the big companies created thousands of jobs. Not many years before, Saturdays had become a half-working day, and for most workers, their tasks finished between noon and 2 p.m. Davies' foresight could see that those thousands of workers could enjoy top-class football, which offered them relaxation and entertainment after the rigours of a hard week's work. This was what Davies was after all the time.

In 1904, as a promise to his wife when he had married her, he purchased Moseley Hall in Cheadle – not to be confused with Moseley Old Hall that was in the same area. Moseley Hall was built around 1800 by the Fowden family and in 1857 Reginald Fowden sold the land and buildings to a Manchester wine and spirit merchant named J. H. Deakin. It is not known if Davies bought the land and buildings from Deakin, but being a keen antiquarian and lover of old buildings it is almost certain that Davies restored a lot of the structure and was responsible for adding the half-timbered cladding, and renaming the building, Moseley Hall.

The Davies family lived there until 1925. Amy Davies re-purchased Moseley Hall in 1935 and in 1940 it was seconded by the fire service. In 1946 it was purchased by the Cheshire County Council and became Cheadle's first grammar school. The school eventually purchased a larger property and the site was demolished in 1987 to facilitate the building of the Village Hotel and Leisure Centre.

John Henry Davies only lived at Bramall Hall for two years until his death in 1927.

The hall is a magnificent example of Tudor architecture and the building dates back to the thirteenth century. Surrounded by magnificent parkland, this location is well worth a visit. The Manor was in the hands of the Davenport family for more than 500 years until it was purchased by Thomas Nevill, a local industrialist whose wealth came from calico printing, for his son Charles. While living in the house, Charles Nevill carried out substantial restoration and remodelling, making the interior more comfortable while retaining most of the building's external features. The landscape of the grounds was redesigned, and a new stable was built along with a west and east lodge, housing the coachman and head gardener respectively.

Another building, known as Hall Cottage, was also built in the vicinity, and housed the Sidebottom family. Thomas Nevill, Charles's nephew and adopted son, inherited the estate in 1916 but decided to sell it following financial difficulties after the First World War. In 1923, many items of furniture were auctioned off, but there was no interest in purchase of the house.

During that decade rumours arose that Bramall would be dismantled and transported to the United States; this may have been popularised by the autobiography of Kate Douglas Wiggin that described the author's visit to Bramall in 1890. In 1925, the house was auctioned, with the condition that if no purchaser came forward it would be demolished and the materials sold off. At one point the neighbouring local authority, Stockport County Borough Council, offered to buy the estate, but Nevill rejected their offer as 'unacceptable'.

The auction received no acceptable offers. However, one of those present was John Henry Davies who later offered £15,000 (about £634,000 as of 2012) for the house; this was accepted. After John Henry passed away in 1927, his widow Amy remained there until 1935 until she sold it to Hazel Grove and Bramhall Urban District Council for £14,360 (worth about £739,000 as of 2012) with the intention that the house and park be open to the public. John Henry Davies contributed so much to Manchester United Football Club and without his business acumen and knowledge, Manchester United could so easily have slipped into oblivion.

For the Village Hotel

Exit the M60 at Junction Three and turn left at the junction with the A34. Follow until first set of traffic lights and turn left into Gatley Road. Follow road into Cheadle village and turn right at junction with Wilmslow Road (A5149). Follow the road for approx ¾ mile and the Village Hotel is on the left-hand side.

For Bramhall Hall

From Stockport town centre travel south along Wellington Road South (A6) to Bramhall Lane (A5102) and turn right (at the Blossoms public house). This road changes into Bramhall Lane South. Carry on along this road – follow the historic signposts (brown in colour). You will turn right down Bramhall Park Road. Look out for Hall Road where you will turn left. This road takes you to the hall's two car parks. The second car park is nearer to the hall's entrance.

James W. Gibson

Season 1930/31 saw Manchester United relegated to the Second Division of the Football League. Bills were left lying unpaid and improvements to the playing staff were something that could certainly not be contemplated, with secretary-manager Walter Crickmer uncertain as to what the future held for his club.

With only six victories from the first twenty fixtures of season 1931/32 and the club in fifteenth place, five points off the bottom, Crickmer decided that something had to be done sooner rather than later and made the decision to approach James Gibson, a local businessman, who had a thriving enterprise in the manufacturing of uniforms for various services.

Cap in hand, the United secretary visited the Gibson home and said his piece, which must have been well rehearsed, as he was to leave with a guarantee of £2,000 to aid the club. Debts were paid and turkeys procured for the United players, who had visions of a far from happy Christmas.

James Gibson did much more than simply give Manchester United a 'donation', as he promised further help, both financial and in the form of experience from a business point of view. All he asked in return was to become chairman and president of the club.

Without a manager, Gibson brought in A. Scott Duncan, the first from north of the Border, who took them back into the top flight, albeit after a near scare of relegation to the Third Division which was only diverted on the final day of season 1934/35.

But perhaps James Gibson's biggest contribution to the Manchester United cause, apart from the financial side of things, was his meeting with his able assistant Crickmer which led to the formation of the MUJACs – the Manchester United Junior Athletic Club, during 1936/37, the forerunners of the youth team of today.

The resting place of
Mr James W. Gibson in Hale
Cemetery, Altrincham.

With cash flow still something of a problem, new players had to come from somewhere and it was decided that if they could not buy them, then they would simply rear their own, recruiting the best youngsters available and developing them through the various competitive levels until they were good enough for the first team.

Not all of course would make the grade, but it was a production line that was to produce the likes of Duncan Edwards, Bobby Charlton, George Best and Ryan Giggs.

Under Gibson's leadership, United eventually flourished, with his appointment of Matt Busby as manager immediately after the Second World War, bringing the real turning point in the club's fortunes with success in both the FA Cup and the League. Sadly, James Gibson was never to see his club's first post-war title triumph, as he died in September 1951, just as that championship-winning campaign was getting underway.

The family connection, however, lived on; his son Alan became a member of the board, going on to serve as vice chairman and later, vice president. But the Gibson era was to finally come to an end when Alan died in July 1995, the name disappearing from the list of office bearers, but certainly not from the club's history, as without James W. Gibson, it is quite possible that we would not have the Manchester United that we have today.

James W. Gibson is buried in Hale Cemetery, Hale Road, Altrincham, WA15 8DF.

Harold Hardman

Like that of James Gibson and John Henry Davies, the name Harold Hardman will probably mean nothing to the vast amjority of present-day Manchester United followers. But here we have a man who gave Manchester United Football Club devoted service for over fifty years: a man who won Olympic gold.

Born in Kirkmanshulme, Manchester on 4 April 1882, he began his footballing career with Blackpool in 1900, as an eighteen-year-old amateur, playing in their first ever fixture at Bloomfield Road.

Continuing his studies as a solicitor, Hardman served the 'Seasiders' for three years and his performances did not go unnoticed, with Everton securing his services in May 1903. He was soon stepping up from their reserve side to that of the first team and went on to play 130 games for the Merseyside club, scoring twenty-five goals. He was also a member of the Everton side who won the FA Cup in 1906, defeating Newcastle United 1-0 at Crystal Palace. The following year he made a second FA Cup final appearance, but on this occasion it was a runners up medal he took home.

Between 1905 and 1908, he was to win four full England caps, scoring against Ireland in 1907, while also representing Great Britain in the 1908 Olympic Games, winning a gold medal in their 2-0 defeat of Denmark at London's White City. In August 1908 he returned to Manchester and played four games for United in the early months of the 1908/09 season, lining up alongside legendary names such as Meredith, Roberts and Turnbull. Noticing that Bradford City were struggling in the First Divison, he offered his services, playing twenty games for the Yorkshire club before joining Stoke City in February 1910. During his time with Stoke, he was invited to join the United board and remained a member until 1931, when he resigned due to club difficulties. Three years later, at the request of Mr James Gibson, he returned and was to succeed him as chairman in 1951.

As well as serving United, he held positions within the FA, the Lancashire FA and the Central League and in 1949 he received a long service medal for twenty-one years as treasurer with the

Left: The resting place of former Manchester United chairman Harold Hardman in Sale.

Inset: Harold Hardman.

Lancashire FA. He died in Sale, at the age of eighty-three, on 9 June 1965, shortly after United had been crowned First Division champions.

Harold Hardman is buried in Sale Cemetery, Marsland Road, Sale, Cheshire, M33 7UN (Grave AC 69 in the large main cemetery), but sadly when his grave was visited in the process of researching this book, it was found in a state of neglect, as the photograph above shows. Hopefully by the time you read this, or indeed visit the grave of this notable figure in the history of Manchester United, it will look as it should, as a lasting memory of the former chairman.

Jimmy Murphy

Without James Patrick Murphy, there is every probability that the history of Manchester United would create a completely different picture to that of today, as this is the man who had countless sleepless nights following the Munich air disaster in February 1958, his mind in turmoil as he contemplated how he could keep the football club going, its manager lying at death's door in a German hospital, with some of his players in adjacent rooms with numerous injuries. Others had died on the slush-covered runway at the nearby airport.

Murphy was born in Ton Pentre, Mid Glamorgan, on 8 August 1910, and represented Wales as a schoolboy before joining West Bromwich Albion in February 1928. Making his debut in March 1930, he went on to make over 200 appearances with the Midlands club, playing in the 1935 FA Cup final against Sheffield Wednesday.

In 1939, having won fifteen Welsh international caps, he joined Swindon Town, but found his playing career brought to a premature end due to the Second World War. It was during his time in the Army that he came into contact with Matt Busby, and such was the impression he left on the Scot while giving a tactical talk to some troops, that Busby's first priority upon being appointed manager of Manchester United was to make Murphy his right-hand man.

Above left: A collector's card showing the caricature of Jimmy Murphy during his spell at West Bromwich Albion.

Above right: Jimmy Murphy.

Below left: The headstone at the resting place of Jimmy Murphy in St George's church, Poynton.

At United, Jimmy Muphy took on the responsibility of grooming the club's youngsters and it was due to the Welshman's ability to get the best out of those teenagers, such as Duncan Edwards, Eddie Colman and Bobby Charlton that United won the FA Youth Cup for the first five years of the competition. But it was after Munich that Murphy came to the fore.

Missing the trip to Belgrade due to his managerial role with Wales, he stepped into the void and, juggling the resources available to him, he took United to Wembley on a wave of emotion, where they were to lose to Bolton Wanderers. Upon Busby's return and recovery, Jimmy Murphy quickly merged into the background, but offering his support whenever called upon. Managerial roles were offered to the Welshman from both home and abroad following his stint at the Old Trafford helm, but he was to remain loyal to United until the day he stepped down as assistant manager in 1971. He did, however, continue to hold a scouting role, prompting Tommy Docherty to sign the likes of Steve Coppell.

Sadly, Jimmy Murphy died in November 1989 at the age of seventy-nine, but his memory lingers on, with the yearly award to the best youngster in the United youth team being named the 'Jimmy Murphy Young Player of the Year Award', while there is a bust of the Welshman in Munich section of the club museum. A blue plaque was erected on the outside of the former Murphy family home in Treharne Street, Pentre, on 23 March 2009.

Jimmy Murphy is buried in the graveyard in St George's church, Poynton, which is situated in the town centre.

Louis Edwards

Louis Edwards became friends with Matt Busby and was soon a face around Old Trafford on match days, but had it not been for the death of Willie Satinoff at Munich in 1958, then there is every possibility that Edwards would never have became a director of Manchester United, never mind chairman.

George Whittaker, the United director who had died in London prior to that last game on English soil against Arsenal, had also vetoed the appointment of Edwards a few weeks previously, but the death of both men left an opening for a new director and on 7 February 1958, he was named as a United director. Upon the death of Harold Hardman in 1965, Edwards took over as chairman, a decision that Matt Busby would later regret, although Edwards did give the manager support when funds were required for strengthening the United playing staff.

That Edwards was at the helm of the club through the successful sixties period is perhaps a mere coincidence. Some might consider it otherwise, but a *World in Action* television programme was to bring the world of Louis Edwards crashing down in January 1980. A month later he died, the television programme doing more than exposing his dealings in United shares.

Edwards is buried in Alderly Edge Cemetery, Grave No. 1712 on plot 7.

Davyhulme Golf Club

Situated on Gleneagles Road (M41 8SA), Davyhulme Golf Club might, for some, be a strange entrant in a tour book on Manchester United football club, but for a long period of time, it played a major part in the club set-up.

Norbreck Hydro in Blackpool was a favourite haunt of Matt Busby's United sides, a far cry from the trips to Dubai of today. But in the days when footballers were simply ordinary human beings, they would finish training on a Monday and then reassemble at Davyhulme Golf Club, where all the club's professionals would either enjoy a round of golf or, if the weather was bad or they simply could not be bothered, they could relax with a game of cards, snooker or billiards. This would be followed by a meal. Matt Busby enjoyed those afternoons as much as anyone, as he found it an important part of team building, allowing those who were perhaps not considered as a part of the first-team squad to feel that they were not being ignored.

From the 1940s through to the 1950s, the golf club was a regular venue, while later on it would even extend into a Sunday morning venue and also the location for the players Saturday pre-match meal.

The Busby Babes

For those who feel reinvigorated by the 'United Tour of Manchester' and are now in the need for more of the same, then perhaps you would like to branch out somewhat and continue the 'United Tour', but outside the city of Manchester.

This part of the 'Tour' will take you to Yorkshire, the Midlands and across the Irish Sea to Dublin, visiting the graves of David Pegg, Mark Jones, Tommy Taylor, Duncan Edwards and Liam Whelan. All the graves are frequently visited by United supporters who have either gone out of their way to pay their respects or have been in the area and made a point of seeking out the graveyards.

In the case of Duncan Edwards, however, it is a completely different scenario, as a visit to the Black Country town of Dudley will take in much more than his resting place, as there are numerous other places to see and all those other locations have also been featured in this section.

TOMMY TAYLOR is buried in Monk Bretton Cemetery, Cross Street, Monk Bretton, Barnsley, South Yorkshire, S71 2EU. His grave can be found quite easily, as it has 'Taylor' on the back of it and this can be seen from the path.

A picture of the Busby Babes' last game together in Belgrade, 5 February 1958.

Far left: Mark Jones.

Left: Mark Jones' grave in Wombwell Cemetery, South Yorkshire.

The grave of **MARK JONES** can be found in Wombwell Cemetery, Cemetery Road/Summer Lane, Wombwell, South Yorkshire, S73 8HY.

Enter by the Summer Lane gate and procede directly ahead reaching the 'roundabout' (two stainless-steel benches on a circle of grass). Carry straight on past this and take the next path on the left. The grave is on your left-hand side after approximately 100 yards (Grave number is 2270).

Red House Cemetery, Woodlands, South Yorkshire, DN6 7EA is where you will find the grave of **DAVID PEGG**. His grave can be found on the central footpath about 50 yards down on the left-hand side.

LIAM WHELAN is buried in Glasnevin Cemetery, Dublin, which can be reached by a number 40, 40a 40b, 40c or 40d bus. When you reach the cemetery, go in the gate on the left towards the

Far left: Liam Whelan.

Left: Liam Whelan's grave in Glasnevin Cemetery, Dublin.

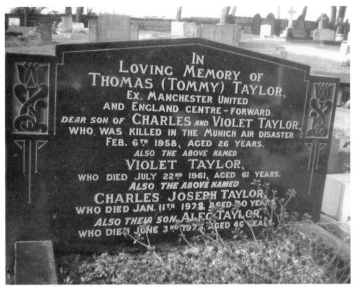

Above left: The grave of Tommy Taylor, Monk Bretton Cemetery.

Above right: Tommy Taylor.

Below left: David Pegg.

Below right: The grave of David Pegg, in Red House Cemetery, South Yorkshire.

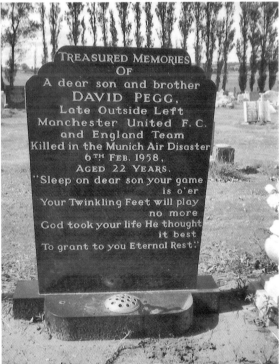

Far left: Duncan Edwards' grave in Dudley Cemetery.

Left: Duncan Edwards.

railway tracks. It is up on the right-hand side. Note, it is *not* in the main graveyard; you get off at the bus stop on the other side of the road opposite the main gate and it is the graveyard at the back of the housing estate. Walk up the lane and it is directly in front of you, about five plots up.

In 2006 Bobby Charlton helped unveil the above memorial at the newly renamed 'Liam Whelan Bridge' in Cabra.

A pilgrimage to Dudley is an excellent day out, visiting the Black Country town where the legendary **DUNCAN EDWARDS** was born and brought up. Obviously, a visit to Dublin and Yorkshire to see the previously mentioned graves could be coupled with a visit to the former homes of those United players, but none, despite their undoubted ability and place in United's history conjure up the same picture, wonderful memories or place in the hearts of thousands as the boy from the Priory estate. Visiting Duncan's grave and finding it without flowers or even a Manchester United scarf, is something of a rare occurance, as it must be one of the most visited graves in the country, such is the reverence with which he is held.

Dudley Cemetery is located on Stourbridge Road (DY1 2DA), and when you enter through the cemetery gates either by car or on foot, walk straight up the main drive (towards the lodge building). Then, take the first path on the left and carry straight on. Take the next path on your left, which will take you down a sloping path. On the right-hand side of this path you will see a water tap. The grave of Duncan Edwards is located directly behind the water tap.

The headstone is quite large, compared to many within the graveyard and can be spotted quite easily. While in that part of the town, Duncan Edwards Close is just across the road from the cemetery.

Continuing on the Duncan Edwards Trail, there is of course the imposing statue in the town's Market Place. Commissioned by Dudley Council and sculptured by James Butler RA, the statue was unveiled on Thursday 14 October 1999, by his mother, Mrs Sarah Edwards and his former United and England colleague Sir Bobby Charlton. A short dedication in honour of Duncan and

Right: The imposing statue of Duncan Edwards in Dudley's town centre.

Below: The stained-glass windows of St Francis' church, Stourbridge Road in Dudley.

the commemorative statue by the Reverend Geoffrey Johnston, the vicar of St Francis's church, Dudley followed.

For a number of years, the Dudley Leisure Centre displayed Duncan's collection of medals, international caps and shirts and numerous other items relating to him. The collection has thankfully now moved to the Dudley Museum and Art Gallery, as upon my last visit to the leisure centre the items were covered in dust.

Situated in St James Road, Dudley, DY1 1HU, the display includes all the items previously mentioned, along with several portraits of Duncan, newspaper articles and a miniature statue.

Another 'must see' are the two stained-glass windows dedicated to Duncan in St Francis' church, Laurel Road, Dudley (DY1 3EZ). The church is obviously kept closed and there are perspex covers on the outside of the windows, but there are often activities on in the church hall and access can be gained from here into the church itself, so it is obviously best to check if you will be able to get into the church before travelling.

The Urbis building in Manchester, situated in Cathedral Gardens, Manchester M43BG.

The National Football Museum

If your thirst for football has not been whetted by the 'United Tour of Manchester' then perhaps a visit to the National Football Museum will satisfy your needs. From a collection of over 140,000 items, there is something here for everyone, with the history of the game covered from its early years up to the present day.

Opening Hours: Monday to Saturday 10 a.m. to 5 p.m. and Sunday 11 a.m. to 5 p.m.

How To Get There

BY TRAIN
We are a two-minute walk from Manchester Victoria train station. Come out of the station and look to your right; you won't be able to miss our big triangular shaped glass building! We are a ten- to twenty-minute walk from other city centre stations in Manchester; Salford Central, Oxford Road, Piccadilly and Deansgate.

BY BUS
There is a bus stop (code NJ) right outside the museum on Corporation Street served by many different routes. The free city centre Metroshuttle service No. 2 stops at the museum and links directly to Deansgate and Oxford Road train stations as well as other Metroshuttle services.

BY METROLINK
The nearest metrolink tram stop is at Victoria station. Catch the Bury to Piccadilly or Bury to Altrincham service.

BY CAR
Manchester is ringed by the M60, linking to the UK's extensive motorway network. Follow these to the city centre. There are a number of car parks within a five- to ten-minute walk of the museum. The nearest disabled parking is on Todd Street.

Acknowledgements

We would like to acknowledge the following people for their assistance in putting together this book. In no particular order:

Mark Wylie at Manchester United Museum, Mike Holdsworth, Tony Smith, Mike Thomas, Paul Griffin, Manchester Cemeteries, Trafford Council, Gary James, Peter Bolton, John Consterdine, Ian Stirling, Jimmy Murphy Jnr, Anthony Parkes, Alan Tonge, Angus Mitchell.

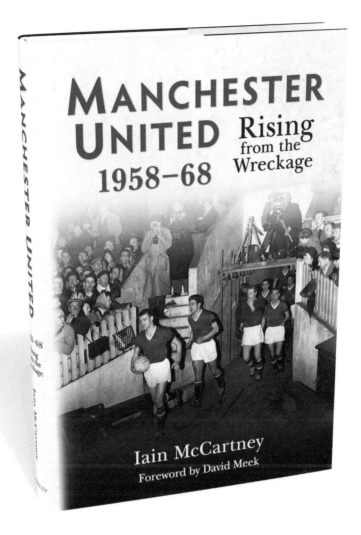